NOTEBOOKS

1951 – 1959

NOTEBOOKS

1951 – 1959

By *Albert Camus*

TRANSLATED FROM THE FRENCH,
WITH AN INTRODUCTION AND AFTERWORD, BY
RYAN BLOOM

IVAN R. DEE · *CHICAGO*

2008

FIRST AMERICAN EDITION

First published in France in 1989 under the title *Carnets Tome III: Mars 1951–Décembre 1959* by Editions Gallimard.

www.ivanrdee.com

Library of Congress Cataloging-in-Publication Data:
Camus, Albert, 1913–1960.
    [Carnets. English. Selections]
    Notebooks, 1951–1959 / Albert Camus ; translated by Ryan Bloom.
        p. cm.
    ISBN-13: 978-1-56663-775-6 (cloth : alk. paper)
    ISBN-10: 1-56663-775-9 (cloth : alk. paper)
        1. Camus, Albert, 1913–1960—Notebooks, sketchbooks, etc. I. Bloom,
Ryan, 1980– II. Title.
    PQ2605.A3734Z5213 2008
    848'.91403—dc22   2007045773

ACKNOWLEDGMENTS

MY PROFOUND, deepest gratitude goes to Dr. Hassan Hodjati for his immense and invaluable aide with this manuscript: *Je ne saurais jamais assez vous remercier.* To my parents, without whom: nothing. To Herbert Lottman and Oliver Todd for their exquisite biographies of Camus. And to Francine and Keivan Hodjati, Ariane Bernard, Véronique de Crombrugghe, Christen Aragoni, and Thomas Field, all of whom have helped improve this text. Any existing imperfections are, of course, my own.

R. B.

Paris
June 2007

TRANSLATOR'S NOTE

A WRITER'S NOTEBOOK is a peculiar thing. To look at a writer's raw notebooks, his unpolished jottings, is to see a man, to know his works, and to watch them grow. It is to get a taste of the life, the human being, behind the books and essays, even when that person has seemingly tried not to reveal himself.

Some might contend that Camus always intended to publish his *cahiers* (as he called them), or, at the very least, that by 1954 the thought had crossed his mind when he began to have formal typescripts made of the first seven volumes. Whether it proves intent or not, we do know that Camus corrected these seven typescripts as they were being prepared. In the United States, after his death, the first six of these *cahiers* were published in two volumes, *Notebooks 1935–1942* and *Notebooks 1942–1951*. Of the *cahiers* contained in those previous volumes, some were fully corrected by the author and some only partially corrected in various stages and drafts. In this third and final volume of Camus' *Notebooks*, only the very first *cahier* (VII) was made into a typescript while the author was still living, and even this one was only partially corrected by the author before his death.

As established in the original French edition, the rest of what follows—*cahiers*, letters, and notes—was taken straight from the original handwritten source, unadulterated, unaltered save for a few proper names. Thus these final *cahiers* presented a series of translation challenges not fully present in the two earlier volumes. Throughout the manuscript, occasionally there occurs a word or series of words that Camus' small, tight script renders completely illegible; over the years many have joked that only four people could ever read his handwriting: his wife, his lover, his daughter, and Camus himself (and sometimes even they had to use a magnifying glass to do so). Similarly, in some spots Camus' script seems decipherable, but certainty is impossible; these occurrences have been recorded with the note "questionable reading" or "unclear word," to indicate the possibility of alternative interpretations. One can assume what they will about the earlier *Notebooks*, but these last volumes, as evidenced, come to us in the raw.

This being the case, I have gone to great lengths to try to preserve the manner of these last notebooks accurately in their translation into English. These entries are not always solid pieces of polished prose; they are often notes at the rudimentary level, they do not always contain complete sentences or thoughts, and they are indeed often ambiguous. Occasionally an entry will trail off, or words will be dropped in a sort of shorthand; sometimes Camus has "dinner with B.M." and sometimes just "Dinner B.M." Sometimes we read of *The Fall* or *The Possessed*, and sometimes just of Fall or Possessed. Occasionally we get long, complex, intricate sentences, and at other times short, clipped, elliptical sentences. These differences, though sometimes slight, are clearly present in the original French, and when possible they have been maintained in the English translation.

Although, for the sake of clarity, grammar and punctuation have been edited in places, for the most part, even when an entry appears less than grammatically perfect, even when a question mark or quotation mark is missing, as long as this is how Camus recorded the original entry, no changes have been made for the English translation. The intent of this precision is to lend a certain authenticity to the true flavor of these last notebooks, sometimes seemingly composed, other times apparently only cryptic notes the author himself would fully understand.

That said, the greatest liberty taken with this translation involves the insertion of commas, without which many of these entries would prove quite difficult to read and decipher. An examination of Camus' handwritten drafts, even of formal works such as *Le Premier Homme*, reveals that the author often eschewed spaces, commas, and even periods. While fidelity has been held as an essential ingredient in translating the particular manner of these writings, in certain places clarity, at the sentence level, seemed just as necessary.

Finally, all the quotations cited here by Camus have been translated from the French version that he recorded in these *cahiers*, not from their original source language. In the case of quotations originally appearing in English, often their French counterparts contain slight differences in wording and structure, differences that have been preserved here as Camus wrote them.

Translating these *cahiers* has been an incredible journey, an incredible insight into the final years of one of the French language's most enduring writers, a voice still so relevant today, perhaps even more so than in the past. My sincere hope is simply that you will enjoy these final pages and final thoughts, this final and most personal glimpse, as much as I did.

EDITORS' NOTE

[from the French edition]

THIS THIRD VOLUME of the *Notebooks* includes *cahiers* VII, VIII, and IX, kept by Albert Camus from March 1951 until his death. *Cahier* VII, from March 1951–July 1954, was typed up while the author was still living and was partially corrected by him. This is undoubtedly the reason *cahier* VII contains passages that are not in the original manuscript. On the other hand, certain pages of the manuscript were removed, undoubtedly by the author, in the typed version.

In the following notebooks, a notation has been made each time one or more words could not be deciphered. In addition, for understandable reasons, we have removed some proper names and changed some initials.

INTRODUCTION

AS THIS final volume of his *Notebooks* begins, Albert Camus is completing what would become his most controversial book, *L'Homme Révolté* (*The Rebel*). Its publication in October 1951, seven months after this volume opens, sets off a polemic so aggressive that its effects, both political and personal, reverberate throughout the remainder of Camus' life.

The most widely noted result of the publication of *L'Homme Révolté* is the quarrel with Sartre, which rapidly and very publicly unfolded in the pages of *Les Temps Modernes* in the summer of 1952. By September of that year, newspapers such as *Le Monde* and *Samedi-Soir* were already labeling the Camus-Sartre break "official."

In December, still reeling from the *Temps Modernes* polemic, Camus returned home to Algeria, visiting the southern part of the country which he had never before seen. Although earlier in the year he had already begun to sketch ideas for a short-story collection tentatively titled *Nouvelles de l'exil*, it was undoubtedly in Laghouat that the story "La Femme adultère" took shape.

Before returning to Paris, Camus met with the French actor Marcel Herrand in Nice. Herrand was again set to direct the Festival d'Angers, as he had the year before, but, terminally ill with cancer, he died just days before the festival

Introduction

began, leaving Camus to take his place. Although thrown
into the experience, one can assume Camus enjoyed the positive critical reaction, as four years later, in June 1957, he returned to the festival, this time directing his own *Caligula* as
well as Lope de Vega's *Le Chaevalier d'Olmedo*.

It was around this time, the fall of 1953, that Camus'
wife, Francine, fell into a serious and lasting depression,
probably, at least in part, as a result of Camus' infidelity,
which was fairly public in France and not at all a secret
from Francine. Although, if by most accounts, he tried not
to openly expose his wife to his philandering, he also did little to successfully conceal it.

On November 7, 1953, in his own cloud of depression,
Camus turned forty. Less than a month earlier, *Actuelles II*,
Camus' latest collection of essays, letters, and speeches,
had been published by Gallimard, receiving generally warm
yet unenthusiastic reviews, which did little to lift his spirits.
In mid-1954 the last of his "lyrical essay" collections, *L'Été*,
was published.

In October, over the course of four days, Camus visited
the Netherlands, spending a day in The Hague and two days
in Amsterdam, the city that would become the setting of his
last completed novel, *La Chute*. During the final months of
his life, Camus had been planning a return trip to the
Netherlands to scout locations for a possible television
adaptation of the novel, but the trip, and the adaptation,
would never be made.

In November, as fighting in Algeria escalated, Camus became more and more anguished over the state of his homeland, escaping to Italy on the invitation of the Italian Cultural Association, a trip that is well documented in
Notebook VIII. Not long after this trip, in April 1955, Camus
took his first, long awaited, vacation to Greece, also well
described in these pages. Upon his return to Paris in mid-

May, he accepted a job with *L'Express*, a weekly journal, but it was short-lived: in February 1956, with tensions concerning Algeria tightening throughout France, Camus quit the paper and focused on finishing *La Chute*.

Shortly before ceasing his work for *L'Express*, on January 22 Camus launched his "Appeal for a Civil Truce" in Algeria. As he notes in these pages, even if he found some peace in being "in the struggle," the atmosphere in Algiers was nothing less than hostile, requiring him to hire bodyguards to prevent possible abduction attempts and perhaps to try to calm his nerves regarding reported death threats. By May the idea and possibility of a civil truce had disintegrated. At this point, as can be seen in the letter dated April 3 in the Appendix of this volume, Camus removed himself from the public arena in regard to the Algerian question.

In May 1956, *La Chute* was published to mixed reviews. Soon after, conditions at home not improving, Camus moved out of the apartment he shared with his wife, an apartment that to this day bears the Camus name on the buzzer.

In the summer months, preparing to stage his adaptation of Faulkner's *Requiem for a Nun* and unable to cast Maria Casarès—his longtime lead actress and mistress—for fear of worsening his wife's condition, Camus was forced to cast a new leading lady: Catherine Sellers, one of the four women with whom he would come to spend his last years.

1957 was a busy year for Camus. His collection of short stories, now titled *L'Exil et le Royaume*, was published, as was his essay on the death penalty, "Réflexions sur la guillotine," which was packaged alongside an essay by Arthur Koestler in a book titled *Réflexions sur la peine capitale*. But the biggest news came in October, when it was announced that Camus had won the Nobel Prize for Literature, an award that again opened him to personal attacks from his critics. In the last months of 1957, as noted in Notebook VIII, Camus began to suffer from acute respiratory attacks coupled with severe claustrophobia and depression, afflictions that would last well into the following year.

In 1958, Camus ended his silence on the Algerian question with the publication of *Actuelles III: Chroniques algériennes*, a collection of essays and speeches he had composed between 1939 and 1958. He spent a good bit of the year working on his stage adaptation of Dostoyevsky's *Les Possédés*, and that October purchased a house in Lourmarin, a small village in the south of France, where he was not able to stay for an extended period of time until 1959, when he finally began work in earnest on his long-planned novel *Le Premier Homme*.

The *Notebooks* end in the last days of December 1959 with an eerily final and personal entry, likely a draft of a letter to Catherine Sellers, which sees Camus lamenting the failures of his intimate relationships and, consequently, his life.

CONTENTS

NOTEBOOK VII

March 1951 – July 1954

"The one who has conceived what is grand must also live it."—Nietzsche.

Preface of E. and E.[1]

". . . at this point in time I began to like the art of this violent passion, which aging, far from decreasing, made increasingly exclusive. . . . This illness added other obstacles, and the hardest ones, to those that were my own. But in the end, it has fostered this freedom of heart, this slight distance

---

[1] In 1937, *L'Envers et L'endroit* (*The Wrong Side and the Right Side*), Camus' first book, was published by Charlot in Algiers. The author never agreed with Gallimard's decision to reprint the book in 1958 in Metropolitan France, but these lines from 1951, parts of which can be found in the foreword to the 1958 edition, show that he had been thinking about the reprinting for a long time. See *Notebooks 1942–1951*, page 234.

with regard to human interests, which has always kept me from bitterness and resentment. Since I live in Paris, I know that this privilege (because it is one) is royal. But the fact is that I have enjoyed it without obstacles. As a writer, I began to live in admiration of what is, in a sense, the terrestrial paradise. As a man, my passions have never been 'against.' They have always been addressed toward things bigger or better than myself."

Insanity of the XXth century: the most dissimilar of minds confuse the taste for the absolute and the taste for logic. Parain and Aragon.

June 11, 1951. Letter from Régine Junier[2] telling me of her suicide.

The creator. His books enriched him. But he does not like them and he decides to write his masterpiece. He writes it alone and reworks it endlessly. And little by little, embarrassment then misery set in. Everything collapses and he lives with an alarming happiness. The children are sick. He has to rent an apartment, but live in only one part of it. He writes. His wife becomes depressed. The years pass, and in total abandon, he proceeds. The children flee. The day his wife dies at the hospital, he places the final period, and what should announce his misfortune to him only makes him say, "Finally!"

Novel. "His death was far from romantic. They were put twelve in a cell made for two. He choked and fainted. He

---

[2] Régine Junier: An elderly American woman who received Camus and often sent his family packages of food and clothing from the States. She did, in fact, execute her planned suicide.

died packed against the dirty wall while the others straining toward the window, turned their backs on him."

N.R.F. Curious milieu whose function it is to create writers, and where, however, they lose the joy of writing and creating.

For her, happiness demands everything, even killing.

Naturalness is not a virtue that one has: it is acquired.

Response to the question about my ten favorite words: "World, pain, earth, mother, men, desert, honor, poverty, summer, sea."

The eternal voice: Demeter, Nausicaa, Eurydice, Pasiphae, Penelope, Helen, Persephone.

O light! In Greek tragedies, this is the cry of those who are thrown before death or terrible destiny.[3]

Man of 1950: he fornicated and read the newspapers.[4]

---

[3] A slightly altered version of this line appears in *L'Été* (*Summer*), in the essay "Retour à Tipasa" ("Return to Tipasa").

[4] A similar line later appeared in *The Fall*: "I dream sometimes of what future historians will say of us. To them, one sentence will suffice for modern man: he fornicated and read the newspapers."

I have always had the impression of being on the high sea: threatened in the middle of a royal happiness.

G. or the simulator: Believing only in what is not of this world, he pretends to be in reality. He plays the game, but openly, so that it is not believed that he plays it. He pretends twice. And once again: a part of him really is attached to the flesh, to pleasures, to power.

The acceptance of what is—a sign of strength? No, this is where servitude resides. But the acceptance of what has been. In the present, the struggle.

Truth is not a virtue, but a passion. It is never charitable.

Tics of M.'s language . . . : And all – In all – In all and for all – So much and more . . . – You know, huh, you know . . . – I didn't find her interesting – She doubts everyone, so it's awkward. – To say so! You have to see it to believe it – It's unique – When she was to be operated on . . . – Strewn forks and spoons (odd) – It was history saying, well hold on, I will make you pay – Remember, you know, she had a knack – And so on and so forth – In other words . . . – You are being a fool (to her husband who leaves without a sweater).

Id. Augusta, a civilian, to whom a soldier, her adopted godson of war, expresses his gratitude in these terms: "Mme. Pellerin, for me you were worse than a mother." She recounts the bombardment of Nantes. Surprised in the streets, she sought shelter with a friend beneath the ruins. "I was wearing a fox fur and a new outfit. When it was over, I was in underwear." Her friend disappeared beneath the ruins. "I pulled her by the hair, only a few strands remaining." "In the meantime my husband was behaving in a perfectly loving manner, not even wondering if I came out of the ruins. . . . The day before I had an ID card made. I had checked no special indications. The following day, I had a hangover."

A Baptist who passes fifty days and fifty nights in Buchenwald's black dungeon: "When I got out, the concentration camp appeared as beautiful to me as freedom."

"They live as one sole being, those who at any given time, by their own will, choose separation." Hölderlin.[5] The Death of Empedocles.

Id. "But you, you were born for a limpid day."[6]

Id. "Before him, at the happy hour of death, on a sacred day, the Divine casts off the veil."

These are the atrocities of Admiral Kolchak[7] who, according to Victor Serge,[8] gave the Cheka in the Russian C.P. the advantage over all those who desired greater humanity.

---

[5] Friedrich Hölderlin (1770–1843), German poet who suffered severe mental affliction the latter half of his life.

[6] This quotation was used as an epigraph for Camus' *L'Été* (*Summer*).

[7] Aleksandr Kolchak (1874–1920), Russian naval officer, worked with the White Army against the Bolsheviks.

[8] Victor Kibalchich (1890–1947), better known as Victor Serge, Russian revolutionary and writer, published books on communism as well as novels and poetry. It seems likely, based on this series of notes, that Camus was reading his *Memoirs of a Revolutionary*.

1920. Abolition of the death penalty. In the night preceding the promulgation of the decree, the Cheka massacred the prisoners.[9] The penalty, by the way, was reestablished a few months later. Gorki: "When will we stop the killing and the bleeding?"

Victor Serge. "Everything that was done in the U.S.S.R. would have been done far better by a Soviet democracy."

Preface of E. and E.[1] – My uncle – "Voltarian, as one was in his time, he professed the stiffest contempt for men in general and his bourgeois clients in particular. In satire and anathema, he was sparkling. He had character, too, and his company struck me as difficult. Now that he is dead, I am bored in Paris when I think of him."

How the XXth century's socialism expands by war: The war of 1914 ignites the revolution of 1917. Foreign wars, in addition to the civil war in China, give us Mao Tse Toung – 1939 Sovietize the Polish Ukraine and Bielorussia, the Baltic States, and Bessarabia. The war of 1941 – 45 brings Russia over the Elbe. The war against Japan gives them Sakhalin, the Kuriles, North Korea. Also watch Finland and South Korea.

---

[9] On January 17, 1920, the Bolshevik government abolished the death penalty. The Cheka, the Soviet state security force, answered this action by senselessly slaughtering hundreds of prisoners before the new law took effect. In his *Memoirs of a Revolutionary*, Victor Serge wrote: "While the newspapers were printing the decree, the Petrograd Cheka were liquidating their stock! Cartload after cartload of suspects had been driven outside the city during the night, and then shot, heap upon heap. In Petrograd between 150 and 200; in Moscow, it was said between 200 and 300."

[1] *L'Envers et l'endroit (The Wrong Side and the Right Side)*. The uncle is Gustave Acault, husband of one of Camus' mother's sisters, a butcher on Michelet Street in Algiers.

Novel character. Ravanel.[2] Pure intelligence. Accounts of terrorism. Mundane ennui. Militancy. Police. Attorney. See new attorney above.

One must place one's principles in big things. For the small, graciousness will suffice.

The cynical and realistic positions make it possible to reach a decision and be contemptuous about it. The others force us to seek understanding. Hence the prestige of the first over the intellectuals.

We work in our time without hope of true reward. They work courageously for their personal eternity.

No matter what it claims, the century is in search of an aristocracy. But it does not realize that for this it must renounce the goal it so proudly assigns itself: well-being. There is no aristocracy without sacrifice. An aristocrat is, first, one who gives without receiving, one who *obligates* oneself. The Ancient Regime is dead for having forgotten this.

Wilde.[3] He wanted to place art above all else. But the grandeur of art is not to rise above all. On the contrary, it

[2] Serge Ravanel—polytechnician, chief of the French Groups during the Resistance, seized by the Gestapo, escaped prisoner—becomes regional chief of the Mouvements Unis de Résistance (United Movements of Resistance) and, according to Henri Frenay, an "unavowed member of the Communist Party."

[3] Under the title "L'Artiste en prison" ("The Artist in Prison"), Camus wrote a foreword to Wilde's "Ballade de la geôle de Reading" ("The Ballad of Reading Gaol"), reprinted by *Encounter* in 1954.

must blend with all. Wilde finally understood this, thanks to sorrow. But it is the culpability of this era that it always needed sorrow and constraint in order to catch a glimpse of a truth also found in happiness, when the heart is worthy. Servile century.

Id. There is not one talent for living and another for creating. The same suffices for both. And one can be sure that the talent that could not produce but an artificial work could not sustain but a frivolous life.

Novel. C. and her flowery dress. Evening prairies. Oblique light.

I began with works in which time was denied. Little by little I rediscovered the source of time—and maturing. The work itself will be a long maturing.

They wanted to repudiate beauty and nature simply for the profit of intelligence and its conquering powers. Faust wanted to have Euphorion without Helen. The marvelous child is no more than a deformed monster, the homunculus of a glass jar. In order for Euphorion to be born, neither Faust without Helen nor Helen without Faust.[4]

Revolt, true crucible of the gods. But it also forms idols.

[4] Note for "Défense de L'Homme révolté" ("Defense of The Rebel"). See Goethe, *Faust II*.

Revolting death. The history of mankind is the history of the myths with which it covers up reality. For two centuries, the disappearance of traditional myths has shook history as death has become without hope. And yet there is no human reality if in the end there is no acceptance of death without hope. It is the acceptance of this limit, without blind resignation, in the tension of all one's being that coincides with balance.

Novel. A nice day. "Along the Croisette, she staggered on her high heels. She looked at herself in the mirror again and again before she left the room. Of course her soft flannel pants were a bit too tight. And her hips were visibly wider than her shoulders. So what, real women are that way. Too much chest also, yet, this was not a problem, and really, all in all, it was more feminine. These bodies that were playing volleyball on the beach, their lower halves had to be observed carefully in order to figure out whether they belonged to a man or a woman."

"The small black silhouette paced before the sea. Between scarf and sunglasses, one could barely make out two lines drawn on by a paintbrush in the spot where there had formerly been eyebrows, and the white and oily space of the forehead that tried in vain to frown at the sun's glare."

Short act about the seducer.

No, I don't drink water – Eat – I don't eat much. If I drink occasionally it's because of hygiene.

What does love add to desire? One thing inestimable: friendship.

I don't seduce, I surrender.

Why women? I cannot stand the company of men. They flatter or they judge. I can stand neither of the two.

At midnight, nothing: the commander doesn't come. The seducer is sad. He is leaving. "Come on," Anna says. "No, one cannot be right and be happy the same day . . ." (he changes his mind). "And yet if you are right, there remains only happiness—actually there remains nothing but the love in which you never believed, never having ceased to believe in your own dreams that you call God." He looks at her. "Then is this love, what I feel rising up in me? – It is undoubtedly that. But gently spread apart everything that remains around this fragile plant. Gently, gently make room for happiness at last."

Novel. One of B's secrets . . . is that she could never accept nor stand, or even forget, illness or death. Hence, her major distraction. She becomes exhausted, already having to live alone like the others, having to simulate the little nonchalance and innocence that is necessary to continue living. But deep inside her she never forgets. She does not even have enough innocence for sin. Life for her is nothing more than time, which itself is disease and death. She does not accept time. She is engaged in a battle already lost. When she gives up, she is there with the waves of water, with the face of a drowned girl. She is not of this world because she refuses it with all her being. Everything starts from there.

Dordogne.[5] Here the ground is pink, pebbles the color of flesh, mornings red and crowned by pure songs. A flower

[5] A trip taken by car in July 1951.

dies in one day and is already reborn beneath the oblique sun. In the night, the sleepy carp descend the massive river; ephemeral torches burn in the lamps on the bridge, leaving a vibrant plumage on the hands and covering the ground with wings and wax from where will arise a fugitive life. What dies here cannot pass. Asylum, faithful ground, it is here that a traveler must return, in the house where hints and memories are kept, and whatever else in man that does not die with him but is reborn in his sons.

It is not true that the heart wears out—but the body creates this illusion.

Those who prefer their principles over their happiness, they refuse to be happy outside the conditions they seem to have attached to their happiness. If they are happy by surprise, they find themselves disabled, unhappy to be deprived of their unhappiness.

A tragedy about chastity.

Novel. V. (and at the same time she was translating my truth): I do not desire anything other than what I have. My misfortune, and my punishment, is to be unable to enjoy what I have.

Id. In adolescence and even a long time afterward, the only thing that interested him in love was the unknown, hence knowledge. And hence, affairs. But an affair is never completely sudden: there is always a beginning, no matter how brief. Very often this beginning was sufficient for knowledge, when there was little to know, and he therefore accepted the liaison, certain that it would bring him nothing more.

Like this they confuse love and knowledge, those who have enough arrogance to believe in self-sufficiency, truly or falsely, for themselves. Others recognize their limits, and their love is therefore unique because it demands everything, and being rather than knowledge.

Novel. A.W., a young American who came to Paris after having fought in the war (into which he had been thrown, a happy student and conformist). He lives in Paris, cursing America and passionately pursuing reflections of greatness and wisdom, which he still reads on the face of Old Europe. He lives a bohemian life. He has lost the luster of American faces. He does not look well—his eyes have circles under them. He becomes ill and, dying in a filthy hotel, cries out then toward this America that he never stopped loving, the lawns of Harvard University in Boston, the sounds of bats shouting in the dying evening around the river.

Novel. First part: soccer match. Second part: bullfight.

Certain nights whose gentleness is prolonged, this helps one to die, knowing that such evenings will return on the earth after us.[6]

---

[6] A version of this line is used in *L'Été* (*Summer*), in the essay "La Mer au plus près" ("The Sea Close By").

A woman who loves truly, with all her soul, in total benefaction, grows then so disproportionately that there is no
man who, by comparison, does not become mediocre, pathetic, and without generosity.

Novel. In an unlit room, nose near the luminous dial of
the radio set, a child listens to the music.

Novel. Two characters: the German friend. – Marcel H.

Even though the absurd is not in the world or in us but
in this contradiction between the world and our experiences, likewise moderation is neither in reality nor in desire, but . . . Moderation is a movement, a transposition of
the absurd effort.

Countess Tolstoy's Journal[7]
P. 45 on T.'s work methods.
T. : "How annoying it is to write."
The Countess, October 9, 1862 (the marriage was on
Sept. 23): "All carnal relationships are repugnant" and in
December, the true feminine cry: "If I could kill him and cre-
ate another person very similar to him, I would do it with
pleasure."
April 63. "The physical aspect of love plays an important
role for him, whereas for me it plays none."
63. "What remains of the man who I was?" T says.

---

[7] These page numbers correspond to the two-volume French edition published by
Plon in the early 1930s. In English the diaries were split into three volumes: *The Diary of
Tolstoy's Wife, 1860–1891*, *The Countess Tolstoy's Later Diary, 1891–1897*, and *The Fi-
nal Struggle*.

Sept. 67. "I am nothing but a miserable reptile that has been crushed, I am good for nothing, nobody loves me, I am nauseous, two rotten teeth, bad breath, I am pregnant . . . etc."

78. We learn that Tolstoy read at the table.

87. He howls that he is haunted by the thought of leaving his family.

90. In hiding, she reads her husband's journal, which he keeps under lock and key.

Dec. 90. She writes: "Love does not exist. There is the sensual need to unite oneself with another being and the reasonable need to have a companion for life."

91. "'It is torture for me,' he says, 'to be surrounded by servants.'"

91. The countess reports that she cannot get used to the count's filth and stench. Id. p. 283 (97).

92. The countess reveals that L.T. is happy only because of physical love.

Everybody, according to her, pities her and considers her "a victim."

Then, quarrels over the royalties p. 81 and 97, 131–137, 216, 145.

P. 88. Confession of double love.

"People who have taken the wrong path in life, the weak and foolish people who throw themselves on the brochures of Leon Nicolaievitch."

"These stilts on which he climbs in the presence of shadows."

97. He leaves the house and does not return until morning.

97. He plays tennis every morning.

At 70 years of age, after 35 versts on horse, in the snow, he attests his passion for the countess, who notes it with astonishment.

Stalin nicknamed by his comrades (in 1917): the grey blur.

At the summit of happiness—and night came to find me.

Nobody, more than I, desired harmony, abandon, a definitive balance, but I've always had to reach across the most rigid paths, disorders, struggles.

"'Certainly,' he says, 'I fear not being dead enough in death and lacking air in the ground. But I reason with myself. If I fear lacking air, it is because I fear dying from it. There are two possibilities, one where I will not die from it and I will continue to lack air but without feeling anguish. Or I will die, and why the anguish then?'"

Novel. Jeanne P. and her mechanical gestures.
Id. Military cemeteries of the East. At age 35 the son goes to the grave of his father and finds out that he died at the age of 30. He *has become the elder.*[8]
The Arabs lying here. And forgotten by all.

Novel. Daydreams in the car on the road to Bérard.

V. I realized that it was true that there were people greater and more genuine than others and that throughout

---

[8] In 1947 Camus saw his father's grave at Saint-Brieuc for the first time. Camus was thirty-four years old. His father, Lucien Camus, was mortally wounded in the battle of the Marne, at which time he was not even twenty-nine.

the world they made an invisible and visible society that justified living.

M. Laughable death at the end of a laughable life. Only the death of great hearts is not unjust.

The Spanish refugees. Domenech (civil war – WWII resistance, Buchenwald – unemployed) Garcia (to whom A.B. makes a remittance of a debt of 140,000 F. "Ah, you, you are like me, you will never be rich.") Gonzales (there are classes—and they cannot collaborate – Rejects all of the boss's kindness – He wants to be treated harshly) Bertomeu: The choir (and then he grills sardines in the office).

James (The Ambassadors). "It is myself whom I hate when I think of all the things one has to take out of the lives of others in order to be happy, and that, even then, one is not happy."

Mauriac. Admirable proof of the power of his religion: he arrives at charity without passing by generosity. He is mistaken to continuously send me back to Christ's anguish. It seems to me that I have a higher reverence than he does, never having believed myself to be permitted to expose the torment of my savior, twice a week, upon the first page of a newspaper for bankers. He calls himself a temperamental writer. Indeed. But he has an invincible disposition in his temperament to use the cross like a missile. Which makes him a journalist of the first order, and a writer of the second. Dostoyevsky of the Gironde.

Novel. "At these moments, eyes closed, he receives the shock of pleasure like a sudden collision with a sailboat in the fog, struck from hull to keel, every part reverberating with the shock, from deck to foresail, and with the thousand ropes and veins of the vessel's extremities trembling until the moment it slowly turns over on its flank. Then, the foundering."

Novel. What struck him then was how few objects there were in his house. The necessary—never had a word been better illustrated. When his mother lived in one of the rooms, she left no trace, except, if anything, a handkerchief.

"I desired, I called for the highest sufferings, certain that from now on I was to find the happiness they contained (to be able to taste the happiness . . .)."

To start giving is to condemn oneself for not giving enough, even though one gives everything. And do we ever give everything—

Don't ever tell a man that he is dishonored. Actions, groups, civilizations can be. Not the individual. For if he does not have the awareness of dishonor, he cannot lose an honor that he has never had. And if he has it, the terrible burn that this represents is like a red iron on wax. People melt, break beneath the fire of an intolerable pain in which they, at the same time, are also regenerated. This fire is that of honor that justifiably resists and asserts itself by the very limits of its pain. This is at least what I felt the day, more precisely the second, when after a misunderstanding I believed myself to be guilty of a truly low action. It was not true, but within that single second I learned to understand all the humiliated.

December '51.

I await with patience a catastrophe that is slow in coming.

My statements on the radio – Listening to myself, I find myself exasperating. Paris makes me like this, despite all my efforts. Since the disappearance of *Combat*,[9] I am too often continuously lonely, having nothing to articulate, defend, expose, or even occasionally justify. Never having been relieved by the warmth of others, and by the spectacle of their generosity even less, I finally freeze, and in fact this frozen voice comes to me, too dismissive to really express condescension, but exasperating to hear. If I felt true confidence, for only one second, I would laugh and everything would be settled.

I owe the idea I have of vulgarity to some very bourgeois people, proud of their culture and of their privileges, like Mauriac, from the moment they display the spectacle of their wounded vanity. They then try to wound at the exact level where they were wounded, and in that moment discover the exact height where they really are. Then, for the first time, the virtue of humility triumphs over them. Poor little people, indeed, but in spite.

[9] *Combat* was originally a clandestine French newspaper created during World War II. In 1944, Camus took over as editor in chief, a position he held for three years before resigning in 1947. All the articles Camus composed for the paper during this period may be found in the collection *Camus at Combat: Writing 1944–1947*.

I was never very submissive to the world, to opinion. Yet I was, however, as little as it may have been. But I have just made the final effort. I do believe that in this regard, my freedom is total. Free, therefore benevolent.

I have the most dreadful opinion of myself, for days on end.

Velasquez's life. Commentary on Velasquez.

Moderation. They consider it the resolution of contradiction. It cannot be anything other than the affirmation of contradiction and the heroic decision to stay with it and to survive it.

The U.S.S.R.'s best protection against the atomic bomb is the international morale that is bound to develop through public condemnations. Thus, it compensates for its only inferiority by an appeal to moral judgment which, however, it denies in its official philosophy.

Hypocritical injustice leads to wars. Violent justice precipitates them.

Marxism makes the same reproach of Jacobin and Bourgeoisie society that it made of Christianity and Hellenism: intellectualism and formalism.

Play. He returns from the war. Nothing has changed except that he only speaks poetically.

Emerson: Every wall is a door.

Never attack anybody, especially not in writing. The time of criticism and polemics is over – Creation.

Totally eliminating criticism and polemics – From now on, the single and constant affirmation.
Understand them all. Love and admire but a few.

The worst of fortunes is a bad temperament. I know this from experience. And this was my true temptation after years of brilliance and strength. I surrendered to it, enough to be informed from now on, and then I got out.

Overbeck had the impression that Nietzsche's madness was a sham. The impression always given to me by any demented person. Perhaps love is also like this. For half, a sham.

The "limit" must be everyone's truth. It is mine as long as I am for everyone. But for me alone: the truth one cannot say.

Guilloux of Chamson: "For him, the other is but a potential switch."

Over the entire world, the arrival of millions of marvelous machines, torrents of sad music.

Judas sets up treason and hatred in order to testify in principle, at least indirectly, for Christ. Result: the XXth century. For lack of love, the camps.

Journalism, according to Tolstoy: an intellectual mess. He wanted to write a novel "where there were none guilty." Letter from a dying Turgenev to Tolstoy: "I have been happy to be your contemporary."

Novel (or play) – Character: Ellan – Fur. Cf. Heliosang.

The myth of Euphorion. The child of contemporary titanism and ancient beauty. Goethe makes him die. But he can live.[1]

Met P. Vianney[2] yesterday, never seen since the occupation and the marvelous days of the Liberation of Paris. And suddenly an immense nostalgia, to the point of tears, for our comrades.

Man of Aran.[3] The terrible life of these fishermen. And far from feeling sorry for them, one admires and respects

---

[1] See page 10.

[2] Philippe Vianney, Resistance fighter, one of the leaders of the Movement de libération national (National Liberation Movement).

[3] Robert Flaherty's 1934 film.

them. It is not poverty or endless work that makes for the degradation of mankind, but the filthy servitude of the factory and the life of the suburbs.

Two o'clock in the morning. For years, two favorite dreams, one of which, in different forms, is always of the execution. Tonight, awakened suddenly, I can recall many of the details.

I walk in torment. Scotto Lavina (a friend from Algiers whom I very rarely see, but like very much) accompanies me. He whispers in my ear (the group's pace quickens): "My wife spoke to me yesterday of X. and X." And I: "No proper names, above all no proper names." He, very softly, as to a sick person, "Oh! Forgive me." Someone in the group (there are guards whose presence is not very noticeable to me, and A., present and absent in turn) asks me why and, reaching the bottom of an immense staircase, I say: "I want to remain at the heart of the common noun," a sentence that I repeat to myself, with a sort of peace. My children[4] are at the top of the staircase, which I climb, always surrounded, always rapidly, and hands bound, I believe. (The idea, too, of being pushed, all of us pushed—we all walk bent forward.) Jean moves toward a corner, and while looking at him, I say: "And then it will begin again" (but this feeling is not entirely in me, rather, like a sunrise, it is a sort of delightful and anguishing discovery). I kiss them and, for the first time, cry. They say goodbye to me as usual, it seems. We leave the staircase and pass by a sort of railway station, which I exit with only A. and Vera. Vera accompanies me for a while—I do not know her during the dream, but when I awaken I think of her as of S. She is dressed as a peasant, vaguely

---

[4] Twins Catherine and Jean Camus, born September 5, 1945.

Central European, like everyone around me. The scenery is modern: railways, construction sites, the night filled with a light wind. Exiting the railway station, I move—decisively still, and without guards—toward the place of torment, with an increased anguish which becomes unbearable. But I sense that Vera is carrying a pistol, old style, which she had hidden in the railway station (whose?). As soon as I am sure of it, I cry out in joy. "Ah! Vera I knew . . . (insinuation: that you would do everything that is necessary for this). How I love you." I take the pistol and the march resumes. We approach a group of men who are working. It seems to me that I hesitate some, as if I wanted to wait longer, live longer. But the others have passed me a little. The pistol is too long and I have difficulty straightening it against my temple. I shoot rapidly, thinking that I have not said goodbye to A. nor to anyone else. A terrible burst in my head. And I hear a sentence, a sort of protestation spoken by one of the workers (the boss, I believe) and whom I have forgotten at the moment when this dream ends.

Picaresque novel. Journalist – From Africa to the entire world.

Play of love.

Your morals are not mine. Your conscience is not mine anymore.

V. "If today one were to find a remedy for death, I would not take it. My pain (the death of his father and his mother) my happiness (his love) has meaning only if I myself must also go there."

Emerson. "Sometimes even the one who supported these doctrines (that man has one soul) flees in the face of a journal composed in the night by some dark scoundrel who knows not what he writes and drenches his quill in the mud and shadows."

Id. "What is left for us if not to hold for certain that it is by avoiding lies and anger that we acquire the voice and language of man."

Id. "It is not with scruples that a man grows tall. Like a beautiful day, height is given according to God's will."

Novel. The train from St. Étienne-Dunières under the occupation, one winter evening. The train is packed, two compartments having been reserved for the German army. Shortly before the stop at Firminy, a German soldier notices that his bayonet was stolen while he was in the toilet. Howls of rage. Two workmen who were preparing to get off and return home at the end of their day are grabbed, held in the corridor while the train departs. They protest, feebly, their innocence obvious. At the following stop, the soldiers let them go. They are seen moving away in the frozen fog, resigned to the worst.

The witness also goes, unhappy. He cannot follow them. He does not know how to save them. He spends the night in the waiting room, thinking of them. Nothing to do but continue on so that this does not happen again. But by then they will be beaten, and will possibly die.

Thoreau. "As long as a man remains himself, everything is in agreement with him: governments, society, even the sun, the moon, and the stars."

Id. Emerson. "A man's obedience to his genius is faith par excellence."

Nietzsche to his sister, with regard to the Lou[5] affair: "No I am not made for hostility and hatred. . . . Hitherto I have never hated anyone. It is only now that I feel humiliated."

According to him, the necessity "against Alexander" of those "who would again link the Gordian knot of Greek civilization after it was severed."

What I have said, I have said it for the good of all and from that part of me that is always visible. But another part of me knows the secret that is not meant to be revealed— and with which one will have to die.

"A labyrinthine man never seeks the truth, but always and only Ariane."

---

[5] Lou Andreas-Salomé (1861–1937), who, over the course of her life, held close relationships with Nietzsche, Freud, Wagner, and Rilke. Nietzsche pined for Lou, but by the close of 1882 she and Paul Ree were living happily together, leaving Nietzsche behind. The above quote is from a letter sent by Nietzsche in 1883, after reconciling with his sister. At the end of November 1882, he wrote to Malvida von Meysenbug: "My sister considers Lou a poisonous reptile who must be destroyed at all costs, and she acts accordingly."

During long moments at Iéna's clinic, Nietzsche speaks lucidly with Overbeck about everything—*except about his own works*.

Genius is health, superior style, and good temperament—but on top of the chasm.

Creation. The more it gives, the more it receives—Giving generously to grow richer.

The only immortal is the one for whom all things are immortal (E.[6]).

According to Emerson, Americans are prodigious mechanics because they fear fatigue and pain: out of laziness.

Every writer, big or small, needs to say or write that the genius is always hissed at by his contemporaries. Naturally, this is not true, it happens only occasionally and often by chance. But this need within the writer is enlightening.

Emerson 1848. "How then did we manage for the progress of mechanization to serve everyone, aside from the worker. He was fatally wounded from this."

Id. "It is every man's right to see himself judged and characterized according to his leading influence."

[6] Emerson.

The Ancients and the Classics feminized nature. We entered there. Our painters virilize nature, and it enters into our eyes, pierces them even.

"No psychology in art." "That's what you're missing." "Perhaps, but such is the law of creation: make do with what you have. Then you will have to judge not what I have, but what I have done."

To remain a man in today's world, one must have not only unfailing energy and unwavering intensity, one must also have a little luck.

Novel. "It can now no longer be a question of love between us. It has never been a question. Deep down, I cried for years after your love – And then I cried only after your *attention.* I obtained neither one nor the other."

Play. D. Haughty, contemptuous, desperate, blunt.

G. is stopped in his novel by the distraction that his wife is causing him. He comes to Paris to work, but gets nowhere. In truth, he does not *want* to regain the thread, to hold on to the argument and preserve his resentment intact.

He executed them with his own hands: "'It is necessary,' he said, 'to pay with one's own flesh.'"

To the few men who allowed my admiration, I owe a debt of gratitude, the highest of my life.

Sexual liberty has brought us at least this: that chastity and superiority of will are now possible. All the experiences, the women kept or free, passionate or nonchalant, and he, wild or circumspect, exultant or incapable of desire, the circle is complete. There is no more mystery or inhibition. Intellectual freedom is then almost complete, control almost always possible.

Project. Perpetual dictionary (for Chronicles). Write *Caprices* (a la Goya).

Deep inside me, the Spanish solitude. Man does not escape from it but for a few "*instants,*" then he returns to his island. Later (since 1939) I tried to reconnect, I repeated all the steps of the era. But double-time, on the wings of clamor, beneath the lashes of wars and revolutions. Today, I am through—and my solitude overflows with shadows and works that belong only to me.

Iguape. A man at the front of the ferryboat. The city, the procession. The man and the stone collapse. The visitor takes the stone but passes the church and walks toward the river. He loads the stone onto a long rowboat and rides up the river toward the primeval forest where he disappears.[7]

[7] Note utilized in "The Growing Stone," one of the short stories in *Exile and the Kingdom.*

Even my death will be contested. And yet what I desire most today is a quiet death, which would bring peace to those whom I love.

One evening, absently turning the pages of an agreeable book, I read without reaction: "As with many passionate souls, the moment had come when his faith in life was faltering." A second later, the sentence again resounded in me, and I burst into tears.

A part of me has despised this era without measure. Even amid my worst failures, I could never lose the taste of honor, and my heart has often sunk before the extreme decay that this century has reached. But another part of me has wanted to assume the decay and the common struggle. . . .

Comedy about the press.
– Moderate? If I find in your vocabulary even one word such as that one, I will kick you out the door.
(On the drama critic) this author has no friends here. You will then try to say this is because of his ideas. In France today, the simple suspicion of intelligence is enough to sink a man. But on all occasions you write that we are the most intelligent people on Earth. The public no longer accepts intelligence except within idiotic commentaries.
The End. The next day he writes the article that reveals all.
The public does not have a memory – We are its memory.
Scene with the reader.
Review of the newspapers: the one that parades Christ on the first page of the broadsheet of the satisfied. Progressive friend of the camps etc.

3rd act at his place. Ascetic.

To the idealistic copy editor.

– Your newspaper is not seen.

– It's read.

– A newspaper is made to be read, but at some distance. One must be able to read a neighbor's copy on the metro.

– Those who read the neighbor's don't buy it.

– No, but they talk about it.

February 28, 1952. The discovery of Brazil, of Villa-Lobos—with him greatness returns in music. Masterpiece – I can only see Falla as that great.

If I were to die this evening, I would die with an awful feeling previously unknown to me, which, nonetheless, causes me pain this evening. The feeling that I have helped and continue to help many people—and yet nobody comes to help me. . . . Not proud of myself.

Medea—by the Antique theatre group. I cannot hear this language without crying, like the person who has finally found his homeland. These words are mine, these feelings mine, this belief mine.

"What a misfortune is the one of the man without a city." "Oh make it so that I will not be without a city," the choir said. I am without a city.

Nemesis. Drunkenness of the soul and body is not madness but comfort and numbness. True madness blazes atop an interminable lucidity.

The press is not true because it's revolutionary. It is revolutionary only because it's true.

Ibsen. (Emperor and Galilean).[8] After Mount Olympus and Calvary, the Third Empire.

Polemic against *The Rebel*. It's a mass collection of darkness and gloom. I read "Tenebrion" in Littré[9] 1) friend of intellectual darkness. 2) Type of coleopteran, a species that, in its larval state, lives in flour. Also called the cockroach. Amusing.

Our cursed poets have two rules: imprecation and intrigue.

The love of god is apparently the only one that we stand since we always want to be loved in spite of ourselves.

Cf. Romain Rolland.[1] Vie de Tolstoï. P. 69. "Life" in the novel.
Id. "It is difficult to love a woman and make anything good."

The Bacchantes.[2] Pentheus should have said: "I do not want your excessiveness. But it is of mine that I wish to die."

[8] Ibsen's *Emperor and Galilean* poses the question: How do we reconcile will and morals on one hand, and love and freedom on the other?
[9] Famous French-language dictionary by Émile Littré, originally published in four volumes.
[1] Romain Rolland (1866–1944), French writer and Nobel Prize recipient, wrote, among many other publications, *Vie de Tolstoï (Life of Tolstoy)*.
[2] Outline for a play titled *La Bacchante (The Bacchante)*. See pages 49–51. Camus once again joins Nietzsche, who interpreted Euripides' *Bacchantes* in *Birth of Tragedy*.

They are rebellion, pride, the inflexible wall that is drawn up in front of rising servitude. They will not leave this role to anyone else—and whoever pretends to rebel otherwise will be excommunicated.

What is it then? One man is waiting to see the most honest newspaper these times have known, created by the sacrifice and labor of hundreds of men, he is waiting, I say, for this newspaper to pass into the hands of a fly-by-night financier, so that he can go lease his services to this merchant as soon as the free men have left the place.[3] The other, at the same time in which he supports and applauds his old friend against me, writes to me that one should not believe much of what is said by these old poets, and, suddenly frightened, writes again to beg me not to make a public statement about his letter and his little treason. Yet another comes to solicit my services, he receives them and, returning to his home, composes an article that is insulting to me and about which he writes to me, incidentally, to soften the effect of it. Yet another, who fears being judged badly for having long represented a publisher who abused my trust, asks to explain himself before me, receives a letter that declines purely out of generosity of not having confused him with his employer and then, without wasting a second, he grinds out an essay explaining how he is saddened that moralists of my kind must one day end as policemen.

They are our champions, our cursed withdrawn beneath the comfortable tents of malediction which they do not leave except in stealth. It is they who ensure our freedom and who announce that they will hold the battle flag firm in the advancing storm. Let us go, the first strike from the policeman on duty will push them to their knees!

[3] Allusion to *Combat*.

Fragment of a letter on The Rebel.

We are very few. But truth comes before efficacy. We must define the latter before worrying about the former. What would be the use of being millions if the first commandment of our "church" were: You will lie? This doesn't mean at all that efficacy has no significance. It has a second meaning. The survival of truth is a problem no less important than the truth itself. It is a problem that comes *later*. That is all. Yet it must be resolved. . . . Christians began by being twelve—Marxists two.

Letter to A. Maquet.

I advance with the same steps, it seems to me, as an artist and as a man. And this is not preconceived. It is a faith I have, in all humility, in my vocation. . . . My future books won't turn away from the problem of the hour. But I would like them to subjugate it rather than be subjugated by it. In other words, I dream of a freer creation, with the same contents. . . . Then I will know if I am a true artist.

According to Melville, the *remora*, a fish of the South Seas, swims poorly. That is why their only chance to move forward consists of attaching themselves to the back of a big fish. They then plunge a kind of tube into the stomach of a shark, where they suck up their nourishment, and propagate without doing anything, living off the hunting and efforts of the beast. These are the Parisian mores.

A certain race of men knows with whom it can take it easy—primarily, those who practice as much generosity and loyalty as they can—and whom decency inhibits from taking advantage of them.

Bacchantes. Two Dionysus: 1) God of the earth. Black God, virile God. Iacchus, a cry personified.[4]

2) The decadent Asian: wine and sensual pleasure, babbling. What Pentheus refuses.

At Eleusis the murderers were not initiated (Nero didn't dare) nor were those "whose voices were not just."

Second day of mysteries: "To the sea, Mystes."[5]

To cross through Hell, Dionysus has to row himself.

3 gods in Eleusis: Iacchus, Demeter (the mother), Triptolemus.[6]

Meaning: death is not painful. It is the terrestrial life that is death; death is liberation.

Rendition in Luke: Let the deceased bury the deceased and you go announce the Kingdom of God.

1st Dionysus will reconstitute Pentheus[7]: "Here is your God, rejoice, but the only one worthy of worshipping me is he who has demonstrated that he won't ever succumb to debauchery of the soul and of the body, to the false god who I am always made to precede. Wisdom now opens up to you.

– Ah! I burn to know it.

– Here it is: you have now won the right to madness. . . ."

---

[4] Dionysus and Iacchus: two names set out for the same god. Iacchus is also the tempestuous cry of joy thrust out in the orgies.

[5] It was the 16th of Boedromion when the cry rang out: "Mystes (the initiated) to the sea!" Each ran to the roads of Phalere to take a purifying bath.

[6] Iacchus is the son of Demeter and her brother, Zeus. Triptolemus, having helped Demeter when she was searching for her daughter, who was taken away by Hades, was sent around the world by the goddess to teach man about agriculture.

[7] Pentheus was torn apart by the Bacchantes, who were directed to do so by his own mother, Agave.

Pentheus and the Bacchantes howl endlessly as the curtain falls.

Also . . . "But wait until everyone quiets down. Listen. Everything becomes silent. It is now that you have the right to madness. For you alone. In solitude. So that it kills only you."

Enter Dionysus II, followed by Dionysus I disguised as a skeptic dilettante (Silene?) "Enjoy, enjoy!"

Debut: the old men run to the bacchantes.

A philosopher (Does he kill? How does he kill? Does one kill well, etc. He who kills so well and I who reason so powerfully. . . . We will do wonders. I will lend him my reasoning and he will kill for me).

A poet.

A priest: what are you going to do with those?

A shopkeeper.

Nihilists.

Bacchante: She wants to go there. Pentheus is opposed to it. "The city must be maintained. She does not have to be sacrificed out of love." "She does not have to sacrifice love."

Dionysus I and Pentheus: Who are you to proclaim so much virtue. – I have no virtue. – Haven't you coveted women. – Yes. – Haven't you taken them – Yes – Aren't you violent? (He hits him.)

Pentheus is quartered. Dionysus II and the Bacchantes celebrate the sacrifice.

Dionysus I arrives unexpectedly.

II – Who can silence the cries of madness?

I – The one who recognizes madness and keeps it controlled.

Id. A man like me, enslaved, if you only knew the thoughts he bears. I have enough rage to smack the gods' faces, enough desire . . . to force my best friend's wife. . . . But these dogs who run one after the other disgust me, each one asking for the desire of the other while only intending to relieve his own desire. Me, virtuous! (He bursts out in laughter) I would like to be the one telling the truth, but my blood is inflamed and my intellect, having all the might, can conceive of all.

At the age of forty, one consents to the annihilation of a part of himself. I wish the heavens would, at the least, rectify all of this unemployed love and make resplendent the work for which, at this moment, I have no more strength.

. . . Every man and woman on me, to destroy me, seeking their share without respite, without ever, ever lending a hand, coming to my aid, loving me finally for what I am so that I may remain what I am. They think my energy has no limits and that I should distribute it to them and make them live. But I have put all my strength in the exhausting passion to create, and for the rest, I am the most deprived and needy of beings.

Novel. "He had no more strength to love her. Alive in him was solely the capacity to suffer because of her, the only thing remaining of love being deprivation and want. She could no longer give him anything but suffering. As for joy, it was dead."

Id. "One could believe that she was all insubordination and it is true that this being, crowned with flames, burned as rebellion itself. But she was above all acceptance. I'll accept dying today (at age 30) since I've had enough joy. And if I were to live again, I would want the same life, despite its extreme misfortunes."

I don't believe those who say we should rush into pleasure through despair. True despair never leads to anything but sorrow or inertia.

Ah! well, here you are, a whore like the others.

Whoever gives nothing has nothing. The greatest misfortune is not to be unloved, but not to love.[8]

Divided between a person who refuses death completely and a person who accepts it completely.

Too many white cells, not enough red cells, and just like the ones eating the others, France too is in a state of leukemia. France is no longer in the position of leading a war nor producing a revolution. Reforms, yes. But it is a lie to promise France anything else. First refresh its blood.

Style. Prudence before rules. They are sometimes like thunder: they strike but do not light.

Boghari-Djelfa[9] – The small erg. The poverty extreme and dry—and yet it is royal here. The black tents of the

---

[8] A sentiment expressed in *L'Été* (*Summer*), in the essay "Retour à Tipasa" ("Return to Tipasa").

[9] In December 1952, Albert Camus visited the territories of southern Algeria by car. "Royal" poverty is an idea found in *Exile and the Kingdom*. Laghouat was an inspiration for the setting of *The Adulterous Woman*. Almost all of the notes that follow pertain to the preparation of the short-story collection *Exile and the Kingdom*.

nomads. On the dry and hard soil—and I—who own nothing and will never be able to own anything, similar to them.

Laghouat and in front of the rock hill covered in folded sheets of flint—the vast expanse—night comes like a black wave from the bottom of the horizon while the west turns red, turns pink, turns green.

The dogs of night untiring.

In the oasis, mud walls above which golden fruits sparkle. Silence and solitude. And then one emerges on a plaza. Swarms of children whirling like little dervishes, laughing so all their teeth show.

Perhaps it is time then to speak of the desert where I found the same escape – From the bottom of the horizon. . . . I also wait to see the fabulous beasts emerge and to find there, quite simply, a silence no less fabulous and this fascination. . . .

Mme V.R. on Malraux going to Japan: "He goes only to come back." But we are all a little like this.

Naiveté of the 1950s intellectual who believes that he must harden in order to grow.

Summer solstice. Short story that occurs on the longest day of the year.

Flowers above the high walls of the neighborhood villas in Algiers. Another world from which I felt exiled.

Death of the concierge.[1] His wife is ill, lying in a large bed. Beside her in the single room, on a small folding bed, the dead body is laid out, which one can see twice a day while getting the mail.

"'Goodbye,' she says, 'my dear, my darling. How big he is! Oh, how big he was. . . .'" We passed the coffin "narrow side first," and upright. Only the neighbors followed the procession. "To think that only three days ago I was drinking mint lemonade with him." "I actually wanted to make him change the gas pipe."

At the cemetery there are four of us. A garbage man gives us each a carnation which we will soon cast over the fair unmoved one.

At Buchenwald, a small Frenchman asks to speak privately with the functionary, a prisoner himself, who accommodates the man: "Well you see, my case is special, I am innocent."[2]

Short story occurring on a day of terrible heat, *in Paris.*

Novel – Deportee. His wife and children are also deported. Because of this, they die. When he returns, the man, superbly intelligent and gentle, dedicates himself to searching for the murderers. . . . He pushes them into a room. He says: I learned this over there—you don't kill someone in the same place where you humiliate them. This is cleaner. There's the telephone. Call. You have time.

[1] Pieces of this entry would later be incorporated into one of Clamence's anecdotes in *The Fall.*

[2] A note later incorporated into *The Fall.*

Play about Returning and Truth.
Scene I – Wife and friend wait for him.
Scene II – He returns and in front of the friend reveals to his wife that the latter was his mistress.

Short story, Brazil.[3] An Urubu snorted, opened its beak, prepared to fly away, flapped its dusty wings twice against its body, rose two centimeters above the ridge of the roof and, almost at once, dropped back down to go to sleep.

One by one the stars fell into the sea, the sky drained of its last lights.

Finally he carries the stone into the most pathetic of huts. Without saying a word, the natives squeeze themselves together to make room for him. In the silence, one hears nothing but the sounds of the river.—Here we are the last, the last place among the last.

– Europe. . . . Dogs.
– Me, too, I'm a dog. I've sniffed and fornicated.
– There is no difference.
– A little. I'm ashamed.
– Ah! You are rich!
– No, not very. But even when very poor, I've always lived richly.
– And it is because of this that you are ashamed.
– Of that. And of having lied, sniffed, and fornicated.

---

[3] This entry, as well as the following two, served as a note for "The Growing Stone."

– Good. There is nothing to be done.

– No.

Id. – One cannot refrain. One cannot refrain. And then comes a moment where one can do no more.

Short story, High Plateaus.[4] The man arrives and his crime explains itself.

"Here. This is the road to Djelfa. You'll find a car. You'll stop. In Djelfa, one finds the Gendarmerie and the train. That track, on the other hand, crosses the High Plateaus. From there, after a day of walking, you'll find the first pastures and nomads. They'll welcome you. They're poor and meager, but they give all to a guest.

The man who kept silent since the previous night says only:

– They are kings?

– Yes, Pierre says. They are kings."

Short story, The Silent Men.

Workmen return to the factory (cooperage) after a failed strike. They keep silent. The day at the workshop.

In the afternoon, the boss's hemiplegia. The foreman announces it to one of the workers. He doesn't speak. Shortly after work, his arms on the table, he cries. "Even that, even that."

Short story in a single fierce run.

On the Pacific. Little mute woman. She didn't know to tell him she was pregnant. He runs with her in his arms. She dies.

---

[4] Notes for "The Guest."

Short stories under the title: Short Stories of Exile.[5]

1) Laghouat. The adulterous woman.

2) Iguape—human warmth, friendship of the black cook.

3) The high plateaus and the condemned.

4) The artist who entrenches himself (title: Jonas).

Then he does not paint anymore. Hands on his knees, he waits. Now I am happy.

5) The intellectual and the jailer.

6) A confused mind—the progressive missionary goes to civilize the barbarians who cut off his tongue and ears and reduce him to slavery. He waits for the next missionary and, with hatred, kills him.

7) Short story about madness.

A confused mind.[6] "Oh liars, oh liars! Me, I know him. He tripped the blind, called the beggars filthy bums. He was nailed against a wall, oh liar, and the earth trembled. It is a righteous one that we killed." Morals were safe. Here he is, head in the wall. When they nailed him up, there was a nail in the wall behind his head, and it entered, like in mine now. What mush! What mush! And then, finally, they cut out his tongue. It is after he had said, "Why have you abandoned me?" They weren't going to let him continue, no one was going to let him sit down at the table, make confessions. . . .

Hatred, I've discovered it. Hatred makes me think of a mint lozenge, mouth frozen, stomach slightly burned. One must be evil, one must be evil. Me, I am a slave, it's under-

---

[5] Five of these seven short stories are found in *Exile and the Kingdom*: "The Adulterous Woman," "The Growing Stone" (Iguape), "The Guest" (the high plateaus and the condemned), "The Artist at Work," "The Renegade" (A Confused Mind). The short story about the intellectual and the jailer and the one on madness were both abandoned. The collection was completed with "The Silent Men."

[6] "The Renegade."

stood. But if I am evil, I am no more enslaved. I spit over their kindness.

. . . There he is. In the desert, the detonation explodes, immense. He has fallen, nose in the stones, head mushy but shriveled. Arms out like the cross, arms out like the cross, I've howled. But at the same moment, geysers of grey and black birds rise into an inalterably blue sky. Far away, very far, a jackal inhales the wind and jogs in the direction of his death.

Finally he is crucified. Our father who is in . . .

How to be forgiven, if one lies, since the other doesn't even know there is something to forgive. One must therefore tell the truth at least one time before dying—or accept dying without ever being forgiven. What death more lonely, though, than that of the one who disappears, wrapped in his lies and his crimes?

Anti-Europe. On the coast of the Pacific in Chile. A little girl of 15 years follows him everywhere with her eyes. She is alone in a sort of shack. He questions her. She doesn't answer, but looks at him. She is mute. Their silent love before the sea.

Novel. "I had long believed, seeing her abandon, that we were complicit in desire. It took me many years to understand that she, and the majority of women, never had any other complicity than that of love."

I've always loved the sea on the beaches. And then the shops proliferated on the deserted beaches of my youth. Now I love only the middle of the ocean, where the shore's existence seems improbable. But one day, afresh, on the beaches of Brazil, I understood that there is no greater joy for me than to tread on the virgin sand in the clear light, full with the whistling of waves.

Novel. Under the occupation, he realizes the extent to which he has become a nationalist by his bitterness at seeing a wandering dog joyfully following a German soldier.[7]

G. Difficult to guess his susceptibility due to his extreme kindness. It takes time. And the whole time one risks offending him.

Novel. Difference of rhythms between people and also difference of rhythms within the same person. D. dawdles in an ongoing seduction. Then, suddenly he phones, travels 1500 km, takes her to dinner, and takes her in the evening.

Indeed solitary from now on, but by my own fault.

We want to live our feelings before putting them to the test. We know that they exist. Tradition and our contemporaries draw up incessant, and by the way fallacious, reports for us. But then we live them by proxy. And we use them up without having felt them.

Novel. "Because of the very same immense wrong he was doing to her, he searched for every little occasion

---

[7] An entry utilized toward the end of *The Fall*.

where she seemed lacking attention, if not love. And then he would give her a hard time, not because he could ever hope to alleviate his guilt, but to drag her along with him in a common condition and still make her live by his side, but this time on an earth deserted and deprived of love."

The one thing that has always saved me amid all my prostrations is that I have never stopped believing in what, for lack of anything better, I will call "my star." But today, I no longer believe in it.[8]

Sachs (*Derrière cinq barreaux*).[9] "One can well live without Catholicism: I can hardly live without thinking of Christ."

Montesquieu quote: "If men were perfectly virtuous, they would not have friends."

Balzac quote: "The genius resembles everybody and none resemble him."

"One only betrays those that one loves."

"One gets the death that one deserves."

"It is not with the people to whom we do harm that we have the most difficulty, but with the witnesses of the affair who pose as benevolent judges."

The tragedy is not that we are alone, but that we cannot be. At times I would give anything in the world to no longer be connected by anything to this universe of men. But I am a part of this universe, and the most courageous thing to do is to accept it and the tragedy at the same time.

---

[8] This idea of the "star" takes on a central role in Camus' short story "The Artist at Work."

[9] Maurice Sachs (1906–1945), *Behind Five Bars.*

Write a stage adaptation of Molière's *Don Juan*.

Play. A man who *cannot hate*.

Men learn little by little to live. And I, for whom life has been so natural, I've little by little unlearned how to live until the moment where each of my actions and my thoughts adds to the suffering or uneasiness of others or to myself, to the unbearable weights of this world that I had, however, originally enjoyed so much.

Tribes of dogs assemble in the city and eat away at the ideas.

Vaucluse. The evening light becomes fine and golden like liquor, and comes to slowly dissolve these painful crystals by which the heart is sometimes wounded.

Couple. There is nothing but demand that controls demand. She only demanded not to die, and me, I screamed toward life.

As he limped, he usually placed his hat askew.

The Russian Critic Rasoumnik in regard to Mayakovsky's *Mystery-Bouffe*[1]: "In the future, historical Socialism and historical Christianity will come together."

---

[1] Vladimir Mayakovsky (1893–1930) was a Russian poet and playwright. *Mystery-Bouffe* was a play he wrote in 1918 about a great flood and the subsequent warring between the "unclean" working class and the "clean" upper class. Mayakovsky committed suicide on April 14, 1930.

As a motto, Char proposes: Liberté, Inégalité, Fraternité.

Progress of the material condition improves more than necessary, and for a very large measure, human nature. But beyond this measure, with wealth, progress hurts human nature. On the line between the two rests the true balance of morality.

Century of serenity. The danger of catastrophe is so widespread at this point that it blends with the mortal future of every condition. This is why to settle oneself with his time today is only to put oneself right with death. This century of the most extreme danger is also one of the highest serenity.

Temps Modernes.[2] They admit sin and refuse grace. Thirst for martyrdom.

Hell is paradise plus death.

Hell is here, to be lived. Only those who remove themselves from life escape.

Who will testify for us? Our works. Alas! So who, then? Nobody, nobody if not those friends of ours who have seen us at the second of sacrifice when all our heart has dedicated

---

[2] *Temps modernes* (*Modern Times*), a political and literary magazine founded in 1945, essentially served as a voice for its original editor in chief, Jean-Paul Sartre.

itself to another. Those who then love us. But love is silence: Every man dies unknown.

September '52. Polemic with T.M.[3] Attacks "Arts," "Carrefour," "Rivarol." Paris is a jungle, and there the wild beasts are seedy.

The newly achieved revolutionary spirit, nouveau riche, and Pharisees of justice. Sartre, the man and the mind, *disloyal.*

The Best friend. Act one. X. at Z.'s home. They speak of Y., X's best friend, who is late. His virtues built up by X. Z. reports certain reserves Y. has about X. The same virtues are little by little denounced by X. as faults. To X., Z. displays a favorable judgment of Y. X. begins to disagree. Y. arrives. X. rushes forward to embrace him. "Ah," Y says, "it's good to be among friends again."

The Doukhobors.[4] Christianity is within. It dies and resurrects in us. Every Christian has two names—one corporal, the other spiritual—which God gives to him at the spiritual birth, according to his actions. The latter name is

---

[3] The polemic with *Temps Modernes*, in connection with *The Rebel*, finds its culminating point in the August 1952 issue, which contains the "Letter to the Director of Temps Modernes," where Camus responds to Sartre and Jeanson. In *Arts*, dated September 12–18, 1952, is an article by Jacques Peuchmaurd titled: "After André Breton, Sartre Rises. Will Camus be the Duhamel of his Generation?" *Carrefour* was a weekly magazine of the right, and *Rivarol* one of the extreme right.

[4] A sect formed in Russia in the eighteenth century, under the Western influences of the Quakers, Masons, and Protestants.

not known to anyone here below; it will be known in eternity.

No, our brother is not dead, but our brother is changed.

Doukhobors. In Russian: those who wrestle the spirit.

Property is murder.[5]

Practical Morality.

Never make appeals to tribunals.

Give money, or lose it. Never make it fructify, nor seek it, nor crave it.

Title: Short Treatise of Practical Morality—or (to provoke) of Everyday Aristocracy.

T.M.[6] polemic – Knavery. Their sole excuse is in this terrible era. Finally, something in them aspires to servitude. They dreamt of going there by some noble pathway, full of thoughts. But there is no royal path to servitude. There is cheating, insult, denunciation of the brother. After that, the sound of thirty deniers.[7]

Fresh water in Oran. African light: voracious blaze that burns the heart. I was too young.

---

[5] In *The Fall,* Clamence exclaims: "Property, gentlemen, is murder!"

[6] *Temps Modernes.*

[7] The thirty deniers noted here is likely in reference to the thirty pieces of silver for which Judas sold out Jesus.

Sometimes, late in these nights of celebration, when alcohol, dance, and everyone's violent abandon led very quickly to a sort of happy lassitude, it seemed to me, at least for a second, at the edge of fatigue, that I finally understood the secret of beings and that I would one day be able to tell of it. But the fatigue disappeared, and with it, the secret.[8]

Brunetière[9] already pled like Sartre for the theatre of situations over the theatre of characters. Then Copeau[1] settled the question with one sentence: "The situation is worth whatever the characters are worth."

Id. Copeau on the "métier," on the "well made play." Not to confuse "revenue" and "métier." Cf. Speech on Corneille's Dramatic Poem.

Every society, and particularly its literature, aims to shame its members with their extreme virtues.

"Love of the distant" in Commedia dell'arte. Princess of Cleves,[2] romantic.

Novel. "In those days it was not her that he hated. There was nothing in her that one could hate and nearly every-

---

[8] A slightly altered version of this passage appears in *The Fall*: "Sometimes, late in these nights when dance, mild intoxication, my fury, everyone's violent abandon, would throw me into a wearied and full rapture, it seemed to me, at the edge of fatigue, and in the space of a second, that I finally understood the secret of beings and of the world. But the fatigue disappeared the next day and, with it, the secret. . . ."

[9] Ferdinand Brunetière (1849–1906), conservative French writer, teacher, and critic.

[1] Jacques Copeau (1879–1949), French playwright, actor, and director.

[2] Madame de Lafayette's 1678 novel.

thing one could love. It was himself whom he hated in her—and his own insufficiency, his poverty, his inability to love what should be loved, to live the way he knew was worthy of her and of him. . . ."

The race that has money troubles and ennui of the heart.

"Wandering in love, loving in various places, is as monstrous as injustice in the mind."[3] Pascal.

Id. "Love and reason are but the same thing."

To the beggar who displays his insistence, the owner of the restaurant, pointing out the people eating lobster: "Put yourself in the place of these ladies and gentlemen."[4]

Novel. Mother sick. So he threw himself on the breast of this crippled woman and cried against her. For years, he had not let himself press against a person like this—had not asked anyone for protection. Some people had allowed themselves to move toward him in this way. But as for him, he had never known how to consent to abandonment. And for this he chose weakness itself and misfortune.

[3] This quotation, and the one that follows, comes from Pascal's *Discours sur les passions de l'amour* (*Discourse on the Passion of Love*).

[4] Published among a dozen notes in the October 15, 1953, issue of *Démenti*, in Liege, Belgium. Also incorporated into *The Fall*.

Play: Lespinasse Élisa.[5]

Act I: 1) Élisa and d'Alembert (she speaks to him of her love for Gonzalve).

2) Élisa and Guibert (love at first sight).

3) Guibert's declaration to Élisa (in a cold tone).

4) Someone announces the return of Gonzalve.

5) Gonzalve and Élisa.

Act II:

1) D'Alembert and Gonzalve.

2) Élisa and Gonzalve (receives letter and must leave— farewell scene).

3) D'Alembert and Élisa.

4) Guibert and Élisa. She gives in to the love that carries her away:

"Have you lost your mind? – Do you actually think?" She turns around, hears him running toward her, and topples onto him.

Act III. Love torn apart – Death of Gonzalve. She is in Guibert's arms; d'Alembert returns with a letter: "He is dead." She reads and cries: "Do you know what he tells me? That he is happy to die certain of my love."

Scene with Guibert-Élisa: "Ah! It is now that I love you," she says.

Act IV. Love misunderstood. She wants to be loved by Guibert as by Gonzalve. You don't love me. Marriage of Guibert.

Act V. D'Alembert and Guibert. Sick. Forbidden to see her. She is deformed. He confesses his love for Élisa. D'A.: "You arrive too late. As do those who are not capable of lov-

---

[5] The life of Julie de Lespinasse is recognizable in this outline for a play that was, ultimately, never completed. A man, Mora, dies of love for Julie, who in turn will die of love for Guibert, the author of *Essai general de tactique* (*General Essay on Tactics*), while d'Alembert, behind the scenes, remains eternally in love with Julie.

ing. The end of their passion consists of loving uselessly at the moment when it is pointless."

Last scene: Death of Élisa. "Did he not also deserve to be loved?

– Yes, Élisa: But you deserved to be loved as you have been.

– Have I been? Have I really been?"

Guibert enters. "Gonzalve!" she says.

Furthermore, I am going to die without him having forgiven me.

Who, Guibert?

No. Guibert made known to me this love where one has something to forgive. But the other didn't know, never knew. How could he have forgiven me?

When my mother's eyes were turned away from me, I could never look at her without having tears in my eyes.

R: Marries a woman who has had a lover (her fiancé). She loyally confesses it to him. He says that he loves her and that this is nothing. Retrospective jealousy. Nights of interrogations and questions. The day after their marriage, he picks up travel tickets to the town where her former fiancé lives in order to "mark his face" (razor blades pushed into a cork). Like this the years go on. He writes insulting letters (Mme X at Mme A's home). Then he forces her to ask a friend to sleep with him. "I'm hurt," she says, then he forces her to ask the same service of her sister, etc. (forbidding her from the country of her childhood where she knew X) etc. etc. Until she is at the edge of madness.

Poems on missing Algeria.

That first morning, more humid than rainy, gave Marseille a Parisian-like pavement upon which a mixed crowd called to mind that another world began here. But all of a sudden, at the flower market on the Canebière, the displays cave in under the December flowers beaded with water, thick, lustrous. Anemones, marigolds, narcissuses, irises . . .

At sea.[6] The sea silently outstretched beneath the moon. Yes, it is here that I feel the right to die peacefully, here that I can say: "I was weak, yet I have done what I could."

Tipasa. See notes.[7]

From Laghouat to Ghardaïa.[8] The daïas and their ghostly trees. The tormented Chebkas. Kingdom of stones that burn during the day and freeze at night—and beneath these terrible weights end up bursting into sand. Even the cemetery of Laghouat is covered with shards of schist, and there the dead intermingle beneath the confusion of stones. Even these meager plowings, which one occasionally encounters in the desert, only lead to finding a certain stone suitable for construction. When one plows in this country, it is to gather stones. The soil is so precious that one scrapes from it the few chips that accumulate in the hollows and then

---

[6] In December 1952, Camus departed for a visit to Algeria.

[7] Due to unrest in southern Algeria, Camus delayed his trip south for a few days, returning to Tipasa instead. The delay was not long, though, as evidenced by the very next entry, in which he writes of the southern cities.

[8] In this entry one can see the origins of "The Adulterous Woman."

carries them in baskets like the viaticum. Water. Soil ground to the bone, to its schistose skeleton. Ghardaïa and the Holy Cities in their circle of ochre hills, themselves garnished with high red walls.

How these stones in the desert, suddenly piled one atop the other, hardly different from other accumulations, teach those informed by poverty the mysterious roads leading to water or dry grass.

Drought in the South—and it's a famine—eighty thousand sheep die. An entire populace scrapes the soil in search of roots. Buchenwald under the sun.

In Vienna, the doves perch on the gallows.

In every job in France, the proportion of foreign workers is intentionally set. This is how the proportion gradually grows in the mines as one gets closer to the bottom. Land of asylum, but asking first for slaves.

A.B. Lucifer depressed about Oran.

Don't forget – At Laghouat, singular impression of power and invulnerability. In order with death, therefore invulnerable.

Explanation of modern horrors through fear. Atom, Soviet trials, etc. The treason of the intellectual left.

Actuelles[9] – 10 French physicians, half of whom are Jewish, without any information beyond the communiqué of the government in Moscow, have signed a declaration applauding the arrest of their Soviet colleagues, 9/10 of whom are Jewish. The scientific spirit triumphs. The same government, a little later, declares the innocence of these still imprisoned physicians.

The desert and the hourglass.

Actuelles. The delegates have refused to give for housing the billions granted to the alcohol producers. Double blow: the slums increase along with the production of alcohol. Six hundred Jacobins, giants of freedom, on their knees in front of the bars.

Humanism. I do not like humanity in general. In myself I sense primarily solidarity with it, which is not the same thing. And then I love some men, alive or dead, with so much admiration that I am always jealous or anxious to protect or defend in all the others that which, by chance or on some day that I cannot foresee, has made or will make them like the former.

Insanity of Fabre,[1] administrator of the Française. He believed that only the world of mirrors was true. The rest was a reflection.

---

[9] Published in *Démenti*.
[1] Émile Fabre, (1869–1955), French playwright and administrator of the Comédie-Française from 1915 to 1936.

58

Benjamin Constant – Diary.[2] "The precision of material descriptions of life has some attraction for the one to whom everything has become of equal indifference."

On Goethe's Faust, damning judgment p. 59.

". . . all people (like the Ancients) who have possessed that which gives value to life, glory, and freedom, have at the same time sensed that it was necessary to despise life and to renounce it. Those who preach to us against suicide are precisely the men whose opinions render life a contemptuous thing, and they are liars, partisans of slavery and baseness. . . ."

"And I am the only one I know who can feel more for others than for myself, because pity pursues me. . . ."

Cf. p. 81. "The men who pass as tough . . ."

"Literature and glory disturb life while obliging in the demonstration and defense of opinions."

"Stroll with Simonde. He reproached me for paying little attention to him and to everyone else. The fact that no one knows . . . that I am not in a natural situation, that my bonds with Biondetta deprive me any thoughts of freely disposing of my life. . . ."

Cf. 133–134.

"Ambition is much less interested than one believes, because to live in peace, one must exert almost as much effort as to govern the world."

"My life runs away like water."

"At the same time, I have such an opposing sense of the brevity of life, that I cannot attach enough importance to things to make a strong resolution, no matter which one."

P. 201. On the uselessness of discussion with the French litterateurs: "It would be necessary to begin by explaining

[2] In 1952 the uncensored edition had just been published by Gallimard.

each point in order to discuss a question; without this one encounters people who reproach only what one did not say, and this is senselessly tiring. . . . It is necessary to write and not to dispute."

"In irreligion there is something coarse and shabby that is repulsive to me."

When a man is generous without affecting those same people whom he enriches with his generosity, he finds that he is doing nothing but his duty.

Cf. p. 226. One conceals one's contempt in vain—it is always felt and never forgiven.

245 – Death of Mme Talma.

– . . . And all these people who call themselves sensible are not worthy of being my companion in adversity, in misfortune, in death.

. . . When one supports a situation that one hates in spite of oneself, the slightest increase in inconvenience puts one into rage.

Cf. 348. My curse is in not loving anything, and that makes even the simplest things difficult.

My soul lives alone. I love only in absence of recognition or pity. Let us not do harm, but remember also that I cannot live from the depths of my heart with anyone.

When it rallies today for the cause of the people, the Church gives the impression that it does not yield to pity, but to force.

Novel. She did not believe in love and affection; she felt ridiculous expressing love.

Cada vez que considero
Que me tengo de morir
Tiendo la capa en el suelo
Y no me harto de dormir.[3]

Play about Albigeois.

Someone writes to me: "In the evening of our life, we will be judged on love." Then condemnation is certain.

She wore chaste dresses and yet her body burned.

Socialism, according to Zochtchenko,[4] will be when violets grow on the asphalt.

Jews, alive as a culture for 4,000 years. The only ones.

Tolstoy writes: "Of life and death." He advances and decides that death does not exist. Thus, his essay is called "Of Life." See Tatiana Tolstoy's journal[5] p 131: Account of three committed volunteers who are executed.

---

[3] Spanish *Copla*: Whenever I consider / That I myself must die / I stretch my cape out on the ground / And I no longer fill with sleep.

[4] Mikhail Zochtchenko (1895–1962), Soviet writer and humorist persecuted by Stalin.

[5] Tolstoy's daughter's journal was published in France in 1953. The journal was published in English in 1951 as *The Tolstoy Home: The Diaries of Tatiana Tolstoy*.

Tolstoy admits that the initial feeling experienced when a beggar approaches your home is unpleasant.[6]

Uttering insults, he leaves a performance by Siegfried.

He detested ignorant and arrogant revolutionaries "who seek to transform the world without knowing where true happiness lies."

February 15, 1953

Dear P.B.[7]

I'll begin with the excuses that I owe you for Friday. It was not because of a lecture on Holland, but because I was summoned at the last moment to sign books for the benefit of those refugees. This exercise, which I was doing for the first time, appeared to me to be something that I could not refuse, and I trusted that you would forgive me this snag. But this is not the question, the question concerns these relationships that you call difficult. On this point, what I have to say is expressed simply: if you knew a quarter of my life, and its obligations, you would not have written a single line of your letter. But you cannot know it, and I neither can nor should explain it to you. The "haughty solitude," of which you, along with many others who don't all have your virtues, complain, would be, after all, if it existed, a blessing for me. But this paradise is attributed to me quite mistakenly. The truth is that I contend with time and people every hour that I work, most often without accomplishing anything. I don't complain, though. My life is what I've made

---

[6] This idea is incorporated into *The Fall* when Clamence says: "A quite Christian friend of mine admitted that the initial feeling one experiences when seeing a beggar approach his home is unpleasant."

[7] Draft of a letter to journalist Pierre Berger. It was published on January 4, 1962, by the weekly magazine *Démocratie*. One can see in this letter the biographical roots of Camus' short story "The Artist at Work."

of it and I'm the first one responsible for its dispersion and rhythm. But when I receive a letter like yours, then yes, I feel like complaining or at least asking not to be so easily condemned. To appease everybody today, I would need three lives and several hearts, but I have only one, which can be judged and which I often judge to be of average quality. I don't have the material time, nor the inner leisure time, to see my friends as often as I would like to (ask Char, whom I love like a brother, how many times a month we see each other). I don't have time to write for the reviews, neither on Jaspers nor on Tunisia, not even to clear up an argument with Sartre. You believe me if you want to, but I don't have the time, nor the inner leisure, to be ill. When I am ill, my life is turned upside down and I lag for weeks trying to catch up. But most serious of all is that I no longer have the time, nor the recreation, to write my books, and I spend four years to write what, in freedom, would have cost me one or two. Incidentally, for some years now, my work has not freed me, it has enslaved me. And if I pursue it, it is because I prefer it above all else, even freedom, even wisdom or true creativity, and even, yes, even friendship. It's true that I try to organize myself, to double my strength and my "presence" by utilizing time, organizing my days, increasing efficiency. I hope to be up to it, one day. For the moment, I am not—each letter brings three others, each person ten, each book a hundred letters and twenty correspondents, while life continues, and there is work, those whom I love, and those who need me. Life continues and, some mornings, tired of the noise, discouraged by the interminable work to be done, sick of this crazy world which assails you even as you pick up the newspaper, finally sure that I will not be up to it and that I will disappoint everyone, I want only to sit and wait until evening arrives. I have this desire, and sometimes I give in to it.

Can you understand that, B.? Of course, you deserve to be respected and spoken to. Of course your friends are as good as mine (who are not as grammarian as you believe). Although I have trouble imagining (and this is not a pose) that my respect could truly matter to someone, it is true that you have mine. But in order to transform this respect into an active friendship, a true inner leisure would in fact be needed, many meetings. It is the luck of my life that I have met many quality people. But it is not possible to have so many friends, and unfortunately this condemns me to disappoint, I know. I understand that this is intolerable to others; it is intolerable to me. But it is so, and if they cannot love me like this, it is normal that they leave me to a solitude that, you see, is not as haughty as you say.

In any case, I reply to your bitterness without bitterness. Coming from someone like you, letters like yours can only make me sad, and add to all the reasons I have to escape from this city and from the life I lead here. For the moment, even though this is what I want most in the world, it is not possible. Therefore I must continue this strange existence, and I have to count whatever you tell me as the price—a little too expensive in my opinion—that I have to pay for having let myself be driven into this existence.

In any case, forgive me for having disappointed you, and believe in my faithful thoughts.

On the theatre.

"Laws" of the theatre. Action. Life. Action and life in great performances. Theatre is persona, character pushed to the extreme. Whatever the situations are worth is what the characters are worth. Errors of conception, of production, and of interpretation result from ignorance of this reality. Relation of style and theatrical convention. Toward great theatre.

Novel. A coward who believed himself courageous. And then one occasion suffices for him to see the contrary—and he must change his life.

Id. He decides to fight against moral temptation. He *voluntarily* gives in to his instincts, which are strong.

Nemesis.[8] Sometimes love kills with no justification other than itself. There is even a limit where loving a person amounts to killing all others. In certain ways, there is no love without personal and absolute guilt. But this guilt is solitary. Deprived of the alibis of reason, it is heavy to carry. It is alone that one must decide if he loves, and it is all alone that one must respond to the incalculable consequences of true love. With this adventurous solitude, man prefers a tepid heart and ethic. He is afraid of himself and for himself. He wants to spare himself, refusing then his condition. And his first concern is to seek a justification which relieves a little of the weight of his guilt. Since one must be guilty, at least he is not guilty alone. Militant.

In love, hold on to what is.

Novel. Theme of energy.

[8] After the absurd cycle and the cycle of revolt, Camus spoke of a cycle devoted to the myth of Nemesis, "goddess of moderation, fatal to the immoderate."

Pasiphae wants the bull by chastity. What it represents is clean, sensual pleasure, a flash of sensual pleasure and not this series of repeated and polished acts, these shrieks, these gasps of pleasure, these pleasures pursued for years in order to accomplish an impossible union. The bull is swift and searing like a god. – Pasiphae (when it enters): O purity!

Martyrs must choose to be forgotten or to be used.

To add to *State of Siege*. Ministry of Suicide. "Impossible this year. The staff is already full. Fill out a card for next year."

Sex, strange, stranger, solitary, which without stopping is determined to move forward, irresistible then, it must be followed blindly until, suddenly, after years of furious passion, before more years of sensual madness, it refuses and becomes silent—thriving in routine, becoming impatient with novelty, and not giving in until the last minute when one consents to gratify it fully. Who, mildly demanding, could ever from the bottom of his heart consent to this tyranny? Chastity, oh liberty!

Honor holds on by a thread. If it is maintained, it is often by luck.

Fear of my trade and my vocation. Faithful, there is ruin; faithless, there is nothing.

A courageous cravat.

Novel. The two sons turn away when their mother, sick, removes her dentures before leaving for the operating room. They knew she always displayed some shame in revealing that her teeth were false.

I have found no other justification for my life except this effort to create. For almost all the rest, I have failed. And if this doesn't justify me, my life won't deserve absolution.

One tolerates oneself thanks to the body—to beauty. But the body ages. When beauty deteriorates, then psychologies alone remain present—and they clash, without intermediary.

There are people who suffer stiffly and others who suffer flexibly: acrobats, (established) virtuosos of sorrow.

Two common errors: existence precedes essence or essence existence. Both march and rise with the same step.

Letter from Green. Each time someone tells me that they admire the man in me, I have the impression of having lied all my life.

For Nemesis. Paris, July 9, '53.
Dear Sir, I've taken time responding to your pleasant letter. But these last weeks passed for me like the wind. I,

however, have been more than sensitive to your sympathy and the manner in which you wish to clearly express it to me. I had liked the veiled luster of your poems, their "lagoon and sun" aspect. And I am happy to sense, moreover, your accord.

Excess in love, indeed the only desirable, belongs to saints. Societies, they exude excess only in hatred. This is why one must preach to them an intransigent moderation. Excess, madness, ruin, they are secrets, and risks, for some, and one must say nothing of them or, at most, barely suggest.

For this reason poetry is the eternal nutrient. One must entrust it to guard the secrets. As for us, who write in the language of all, we must know that there are two kinds of wisdom, and sometimes pretend to be unaware that one is higher. Accept all my best wishes and cordial greetings.

If I have always refused to lie (unfit even when I made an effort) it is because I could never accept solitude. But solitude should now also be accepted.

Like after a long illness when someone whom you love dies. And even though there was nothing to do but wait, it is as though one had struggled long and hard, and then all of a sudden, defeat.

For certain men it requires more courage to face a simple street fight than to jump in the line of fire. Hardest is to strike a man and particularly to feel the physical hostility of another man.

V. "Two values for me: tenderness and glory."

To bring divine grace down on a B.O.F.,[9] or a ruthless businessman—that is an accomplishment. On a criminal, it is easy.

Van Gogh admired Millet, Tolstoy, Sully Prudhomme.

Tolstoy, as a young man, "goes in search of happiness" in Saint-Petersburg. Result: cards, gypsies, debts, etc. "I live like an animal." (Tolstoy by Tolstoy, correspondence – 1879.)

Tolstoy's brother: "He lacked the necessary defects needed in order to be a great writer" (according to Turgenev).

Id. Corr. May 3, '59: "To whom do I do any good? Whom do I love? Nobody. I have neither tears nor sorrow for myself, but only a cold regret. . . ."

Id. Oct. 17, '60, after the death of his brother: "And I've learned from thirty-two years of experience that in truth our situation is dreadful. . . . Arriving at his highest degree of development, man realizes very clearly that everything is a lie, senseless, and that the truth that he loves still more than anything in the world is terrible. . . ."

Id. 61. Tolstoy challenges Turgenev to a duel, but Turgenev makes excuses.

Id. 62. Searching Tolstoy's residence: A colonel reads his diary. T. writes to Alexandra Tolstoy, who is familiar with the imperial court: "Fortunately for me and for your friend I was not there, because I would have killed him." Response from Alexandra to calm him: "Have pity. Nothing in reality is more merciless than a man who strongly feels his innocence and who is unfairly mistreated."

---

[9] Beurre, Œufs, Fromages—butter, eggs, cheese—a derogatory term used to refer to those dairymen who made their money during the Occupation. The term is roughly equivalent to the more widely used 'nouveau riche.'

62. Meeting Sophie Bers: "I love as I never believed one could love. I will kill myself if it continues like this. . . ."

65. "I am happy that you love my wife. Although I love her less than my novel, she is my wife all the same, you know."

Cf. p. 285. Andrey Bolkonsky's outlook in *War and Peace*.

65. On one of Turgenev's short stories that he does not like: "The personal and subjective side is good only when it is filled with life and with passion, whereas here subjectivity is full of suffering without one feeling life" (apply to Rilke, Kafka, etc.).

65. His indifference to politics—continuous—and stubborn. "I am indifferent to knowing who oppresses the Poles."

At 50 years old he still maintains that no one should read the diaries (p. 405).

"During the summer . . . I dream then of death more and more and always with a new pleasure."

69. He discovers Schopenhauer with admiration.

70. Insomniac.

71. On the death of a friend. He does not miss him, he "rather envies him."

72. On Strakhov. "Abandon the depraved activity of journalists."

Cf. p. 320. On a curve where Pushkin would be at the top, Tolstoy places himself on the downward slope.

72. "Ennui visits me quite rarely, but I welcome it with joy. It always forewarns the arrival of a great intellectual energy."

73. To a friend: "Don't stay in Moscow. Two dangers: journalism and conversation."

Cf. p. 366. On the desert and primitive life.

To put an end to her life, without respect for it, is painful.

"We cannot live without religion and yet we cannot believe."

78. He prays every day for Providence to accord him "peace in work." Alas!

Cf. p. 396. Against progress.

What they prefer, what makes them tender and melancholy, what makes them sentimental, is hatred. For each work one has to measure the sum of hatred and the sum of love that it contains—and then one is appalled in the face of the times.

Lope de Vega, five or six times a widower. Today people die less often. The result is that we no longer need to preserve in ourselves a force of rejuvenating love, but, on the contrary, we need to extinguish it in order to elicit another force of infinite adaptation.

If concern for duty diminishes, it is because there are fewer and fewer rights. Whoever is uncompromising with regard to his rights alone has the force of duty.

Nihilism. Little demolishing dunces, contentious, thinking of everything in order to deny all, feeling nothing and relying on others—parties or leaders—to feel for them.

All their effort is to discourage one from being. To prevent the writer from writing, in literature for example, is their constant concern.

Cf. D.M. Hatred of writers, like what one can catch in a publishing house.

Virtue is not hateful. But speeches on virtue are. Without a doubt, no mouth in the world, much less mine, can utter them. Likewise, every time somebody interjects to speak of my honesty (Roy's declaration[1]) there is someone who quivers inside me.

Title: The Hatred of Art.

The artist and his time. Read Tolstoy's marvelous page about the artist (What do we have to do? 378–9 and R.R.[2] p. 113) . . . "the artist . . . he is the one who would be happy not to think and not to say what is set in his soul, but he cannot be exempted from doing so. . . ."
Facing this, "The sentiments of our current society come down to three things: conceit, sensuality, and ennui."
Admirable letters about his remorse (R.R. p. 189–190).

Don Giovanni. At the summit of all arts. When one has finished listening to him, one has toured the world and its beings.

Focused. Sharpened – I ask only one thing, and I ask it humbly, although I know that it is exorbitant: to be read with attention.

---

[1] Jules Roy (1907–2000), French writer who, like Camus, was born in Algeria and wrote of the French experience there.
[2] Romain Rolland.

Too much security for the child's heart and the adult will spend his life demanding this security from people— even though people are only opportunities for risk and freedom.

Novel. Jealousy. "I took care not to let my imagination wander. I kept it on a leash."

"The adulterer is indicted in front of the one or ones whom he has betrayed. But he is not convicted. Or perhaps the most unbearable conviction is to be eternally accused."

Faust. Endymion.[3] The king's death. The ritual – Pandora[4] and the end of the golden age.

Ferrero.[5] "Finally to pick from the tree of life is this small exquisite fruit, so rare from now on, which, over many years, flowers only one time: rest without remorse."

In France, talent always asserts itself *against*.

From Columbus, the horizontal civilization—that of space and quantity—replaces the vertical civilization of quality. Columbus kills Mediterranean civilization.

---

[3] Faust and Endymion are two examples of the myth of eternal youth.

[4] In "L'Été à Alger" ("Summer in Algiers"), in *Noces* (*Nuptials*), Camus wrote: "In Pandora's box, where the evils of humanity teem, the Greeks left out hope as more terrible than all the others."

[5] Guglielmo Ferrero (1871–1943), *Les Deux Révolutions françaises 1789–1796* (*The Two French Revolutions 1789–1796*).

Ferrero. Contradiction of the mechanized world: it creates abundance by its speed of manufacture, and it needs drought to prosper.

Before all else, the natural.

Ferrero. A civilization such as ours, which tends to always increase the quantity of objects and therefore has to always decrease quality, must end in an enormous and brutal orgy. And it is true. The end of the history that our progressive men speak of is debauchery.

Hegel. Moderation: synthesis of quality and quantity.

Without tradition the artist has the illusion of creating his own rule. Here he is God.

Antaeus is buried at the foot of Cape Spartel, on the Atlantic Coast of what is now Morocco.

Ferrero. From Hercules' doors, the Atlantic is an infinite beauty flowing within the narrow human spirit and taking a provisional form there.

Ferrero. The eternal voice that shouts at the artist: "Create works of art and do not make aesthetics; discover new truths and do not make theories of knowledge; just act and do not preoccupy yourself with verifying whether or not history has been mistaken." Id. "Believe in the principles that you profess and don't compromise. But if the principle falls, resign yourself. It will have only been one moment of universal truth.[6]

Cf. p. 354: the power of Society has limits. It has acquired solely through the result of concentration and discipline: the epic Greek tragedy and sculpture, the aesthetics and morals of Plato and Aristotle, Roman law, the art of the Italian Middle Ages and Romanesque art in general, Galileo, Pascal, Racine, Molière . . .

Then the discovery of America, the French Revolution, the machine, the era of production.

But finally it was necessary to nourish the enormous starving multitudes who wander or vegetate on the globe (verify the growth of the human race since the XIIIth century). Perhaps we must pay for this through sterility.

France, which had the audacity and genius to produce that extraordinary French Revolution, is at the same time the country that has yielded the least, out of disquiet, to the madness of production.

Ferrero. "One of these days the act of restrained will is going to explode."

With certain people we maintain the rapport of truth. With others, the rapport of lies. The latter are not the least durable.

Novel. "I have nothing to do close to you. I did not love you enough and you did not love me enough for me to set-

[6] Missing quotation mark.

tle my final accounts with you. I must manage alone and die alone. I waited for years for you to forgive my faults and accept me as I was. You never did. I therefore kept my faults, I remained guilty, and today I must put myself in order with these faults alone. Leave me.

Forgive me, then, the pain that I have caused you. And if you can, forgive me from the bottom of your heart. That is what I need most, though, the privation that for years has prevented me from living. If your heart remembers nothing but the love it has for me, this would be the salvation in death that I could not have in life."

Tocqueville (From *Democracy in America*): "It seems as if the sovereigns of our time seek only to have men make things great. I would like them to think a little more of making great men."

"Russia is the angular stone of despotism in the world (*Correspondance*[7])."

Napoleon delivers the Revolution's bastard child: despotism. According to T, the natural check for despotism is aristocracy.

These minds "who seem to make the taste for servitude, a sort of ingredient of virtue." Applies to Sartre and the progressives.

"What are these people lacking in order to remain free? What? the very taste for being free."

Id. Tocqueville. Ancient Regime and the French Revolution. T. I.

[7] *Correspondence of Alexis de Tocqueville and Pierre-Paul Royer-Collard. Correspondence of Alexis de Tocqueville and Jean-Jacques Ampère* (Gallimard, 1951).

The general idea: it is royalty that created the instrument of the Revolution—centralism—by cutting down the aristocracy and provincial freedoms.

"It must always be rued that, instead of bending the nobility under the influence of law, it was uprooted and cut down. By doing so they have . . . inflicted on freedom a wound which will never heal."

"Democratic societies that are not free can be rich, refined, gentle, even magnificent, powerful by the weight of their bourgeois mass; they can encounter private virtues there, good family fathers, honest merchants, and quite estimable landlords . . . but what will never be seen in similar societies, I dare to say, are great citizens and, above all, a great populace, and I do not fear to affirm that the common level of hearts and minds will never cease to lower itself as long as equality and despotism are joined there."

Id. for our progressives. "We have seen men who thought to atone for their servility toward the lowest officials of political power by their insolence toward God, and who, while they abandoned all that was most free, most noble, most proud in the doctrines of the Revolution, still flattered themselves to have remained faithful to its spirit while remaining irreligious."

Id. "They seemed to love freedom; it turns out they only hated the master."

Cf. p. 233. The main idea of modern socialism—that after the last audit, land ownership belongs to the State—was taught by Louis XIV in his edicts.

Cf. p. 244. In '89 the French were proud enough of themselves to believe that they could live equally in freedom. Then . . .

Cf. p. 245, portrait of France.

The *Notebooks* of the nobility of Paris and elsewhere asked for the demolition of the Bastille.

Chopin (born in 1810). Excellent actor. Refuses the Opera out of certainty of what he is. Congratulates Tallberg who played a nocturne, deforming it as usual: "But by whom was it then?" Prodigal and generous. But pitiless in his dealings with his editors.

In Valdemosa, gulls lost in the fog knock against every pane of the cloister.

Dying, Tolstoy wrote in the air.

According to Montherlant, all true creators dream of a life without friends.

In the Broadmoor asylum, where the criminally insane are rehabilitated, bloody arguments over an empty bottle of aspirin.

Theatre idea (still at Broadmoor): when the wicked one takes the stage, a sign: "Boo." When the hero does: "Applaud."

"The union of three people bound by a gentle conformity of inclinations, virtues and temperaments, represents in the eyes of the Chinese the highest form of terrestrial beatitude. . . ." Abel Rémusat.[8]

---

[8] Jean-Pierre Abel Rémusat (1788–1832), translator, teacher, and orientalist scholar.

Id. "The Island Complex." Two women are needed. Because the man has three souls and the woman four. This triangle is imbalanced on this square. But on two squares, it makes a complete and solid pyramid.

The winter ends in El Kantara when the eternal summer begins. Black and pink mountain. According to Fromentin.[9]

Again Fromentin: small-minded people prefer the details in art.

"Until the last minute of the day, the Sahara remains in full light. Here, night comes like a blackout."

Read Daumas' "Le grand désert."

One cannot live all that one writes. But one tries to.

Kaliayev is wintry love. Victoria solar love.[1]

St. John. "The one who says that he loves God and does not love his brother is a liar; because how can he say that he loves God, whom he does not see, if he does not love his brother, whom he does see?" Compare with the Confused Mind which says: "If I do not love God, me, it is because I do not love men, and in truth why love them?" Id. John. "If I had not come, and if I did not speak with them, they would have no sin; but now they have no excuse."

---

[9] Eugène Fromentin (1820–1876), French writer and painter, who, though not from Algeria, often concentrated his work on the country and its inhabitants.

[1] Kaliayev, a Russian revolutionary from 1905, is celebrated in *The Rebel* and is a principal character in *The Just*. Victoria is a character in *State of Seige*.

Altruism is a temptation, like pleasure.

Tolstoy: "One can live only so long as one is drunk with life" Confession (79).

At the same time: "I am crazy about life. . . . It's the summer, the delicious summer. . . ."

Guilloux. At the beginning of the Occupation in Saint-Brieuc, the city is cold and rainy, the stores empty. It's morning; he walks in the drizzly and deserted streets. Over the empty plaza a German passes, covered in a linen oilskin glistening with rain. Then under the low sky, in the dreadful sadness of the hour, G. enters the church and prays, he, the declared atheist (prays to Mary, I believe). And he reemerges. Every time he had tried to write this moment of abandonment or of cowardice (he says he does not know which it is) he could not, or dared not.

Roger Martin du Gard and his mother's death. They hide her cancer from her. They change the labels of the medications, etc. But after her death, the memory of this terrible agony pursues M. du G. who tells himself he will not be able to bear it. The only possible hope would be to kill himself. But will he have the courage? He attempts it, goes through several "rehearsals" with a revolver, but at the last moment (pressing on the trigger) he feels his courage lacking. Thus the anguish grows, he feels stuck, until he finds the "way." He takes a taxi, brings the revolver to his forehead. "When I arrive at the level of the third lamppost, I will press on the trigger." He gets to the third lamppost and *feels* ready to press on in this manner. Consequently, an immense feeling of freedom.

The same person tells me that he suffers from wanting nothing anymore, not even to live (see his letter). The anorexia about which Gide spoke. In Nice, suddenly a hope. He sees a sign for "Bouillabaisse" at the door of a restaurant and *wants to have some*. It is his first *want* in months. He enters, eats with joy. Since then, nothing more. He is in the waiting room when he writes to me.

Of all the men I have met, he is the most human, which is to say the most worthy of tenderness.

Stendhal. "What is the self? I know nothing of it. One day I am awakened on this Earth, I find myself tied to my body, to a character, to a fortune. Shall I vainly enjoy myself by trying to change these things, all the while forgetting to live. Deception! I subject myself to their defects. I subject myself to my aristocratic tendencies after having railed for ten years, and in good faith, against any aristocracy."

L'Impromptu des Philosophes[2] as commedia dell'arte.

A "modern" title: The Hatred of Art.

Write naturally. Publish naturally and pay the price for all this, naturally.

Criticism is to the creator what the merchant is to the producer. Thus, the commercial age sees an asphyxiating

---

[2] *L'Impromptu des Philosophes* (*The Philosopher's Farce*) is a short play by Camus, recently published in France among his *Œuvres complètes* (*Complete Works*).

multiplication of commentators, intermediaries, between the producer and the public. Thus, it is not that we are lacking creators today, it is that there are too many commentators who drown the exquisite and elusive fish in their muddy waters.

Novel. See Weissberg's notes.[3] At the interrogation, the chekists put a golden paper crown decorated with swastikas on his head, a large swastika on his chest, and then they hit him.

Id. The old anarchist tailor explains his point of view clearly. The judge insults him: "You have offended me, your honor, I will not answer any more of your questions." Record of the interrogation: *thirty-one days and thirty-one nights*. Madhouse!

Novel. 1st part. Search for a father or the unknown father. Poverty does not have a past. "Day in the provincial cemetery. . . . X. discovered that his father had died at a younger age than he himself was at that very moment . . . that the person lying there had already been his junior for 2 years, even though he was 35 years old when he was laid there. . . . He realized he knew nothing of this father and decided to look for him[4] . . ."

Birth during relocation.

2nd part. Childhood (or weave this with the first part) Who am I?

3rd part. The education of a man. Incapable of tearing himself away from bodies. Ah! The innocence of first acts!

---

[3] Alex Weissberg, *L'Accusé* (*The Accused*).
[4] See page 17.

But the years pass, people bond and each act of the flesh binds, prostitutes, engages more and more.

He does not want to be judged (to tell the truth, he judges little) but there is no way to avoid it.

Two characters:

1) The indifferent one: raised without a familial environment. Without a father. A single mother. He manages alone. A little haughty, although polite. Always walks alone. Goes to boxing and soccer matches. Likes only the peak moment. Forgets the rest. At the same time begs of others the tenderness of which he is incapable. Lies easily but has terrible urges to tell the truth. A little monstrous. Secrecy until the end, because he forgets major parts of his life, since few things interest him – An artist by his very shortcomings.

2) The other, sensitive and generous.

They meet at the end (and it is the same) next to the mother.

O father! I have searched madly for this father whom I never had and here I discovered what I have always had: my mother and her silence. The five movements of Mozart's Quintet in G Minor.

Love and Paris. Algeria. "We did not know love."

Id. Poor childhood. Life without love (not without pleasures). The mother is not a source of love. Consequently, what takes longest in the world is learning to love.

Two people are brought together purely by looks (let's say the cashier and the customer). When the opportunity presents itself, they tackle each other. What does he say?

"Do you have time?" What does she say, how does she respond?

"I'll say that I went somewhere."

In two forces of equal tension, progress is an optimum balance. It takes account of the limits and subjugates them to a greater good. And not in a vertical arrow, which would suppose that progress is limitless.

Play. We wait for him. He returns from the camp. He speaks the truth about love (because he has failed: he now knows what a man is).

Scene with his wife, and in front of her, Philinte and G., Philinte's wife. "For example, I slept with G. . . . Moreover, I am not sure that you and Philinte." – Philinte: "No. It's not that G. is not delectable. And although I do not like the truth, I will speak it by way of exception. When I saw that you and G. . . ." – "How" – "Yes, I knew it. From that moment everything became impossible between your wife and me. So finally this continual coming and going—ugh! You agree with me don't you? Then come for dinner tomorrow? G. will make her chaud-froid[5] for you. She is unbeatable when it comes to chaud-froid." End of the act.

But your feelings? – Well what about my feelings? They existed like all things, intermittingly – And the rest of the time? – I was lying, of course. – I preferred your lie – Of course, you've always loved napping – But you're a monster! – And you, my angel?

[5] A culinary dish, literally hot-cold, usually consisting of meat or chicken that has been cooled and coated with a gelatinous sauce.

Id. For example, my son is an imbecile – Ah! that, the son says – You see. You protest. It's the reaction of an imbecile. An intelligent man always admits the possibility—I should say the probability—of being an imbecile in some ways. Thus my son is an imbecile (he looks at him). Not completely, however. Rather, he plays stupid. He is cunning and he knows that stupidity has its advantages, that it is the hearth around which society warms itself.

Id. The son becomes social. "When the social plan coincides with the private plan . . . – Your mother will become intelligent? No, but . . . One does not covet another's wife? – Surely – Why, yours will be perfect? – No . . . – You, I see you coming. You want to use the social force of others to sort out the small problems of your private life. Leave that, my boy. The misery of others is their private life. They will sort out this little affair, nothing to fear. But don't touch. Ah! don't touch.

Id. But he falls in love with Dominique. And again he lies.

The intellectual who asks forgiveness.

"Worst was the Gospel. Yes, I read the Gospel, initially because I only had that in hand and then because I realized by its usage that there were more common points between Jesus and me than between a policeman and me. And today's world is composed for the three-quarters that are policemen or for the policemen's admirers."

A man whose life is full refuses many advances. Then, for the same reason, he forgets his refusal. But those advances were made by people whose lives were not full and who, for this same reason, remember. The first later finds he has enemies and is astonished by it. Like this, almost all artists imagine they were persecuted. But no, one responded to their refusal and one punished them for their excess of riches. There is no injustice.[6]

The First Man
Plan?
1) Search for a father.
2) Childhood.
3) The years of happiness (sick in 1938). Action as a happy overabundance. Powerful feeling of liberation when it's over.
4) War and resistance (Bir Hakeim and the alternative clandestine newspaper).
5) Women.
6) Mother.
The indifferent one. A complete man. A high-caliber mind, a skillful body broken by pleasures. He refuses to be loved out of impatience, and out of the exact feeling of what he is. Sweet and kind in illegitimacy. Cynical and terrible in virtue.

He can do anything because he has decided to kill himself. Cyanide. Thus he enters the resistance, whence extraordinary audacity. But the day when he has to help himself to the cyanide, *he abstains from it.*

The First Man
Search for a father.
The hospital. The mother (and this paper from the town hall which is brought to the two illiterate women peeling potatoes on the floor; he must help the deputy mayor in and hand him the paper so that he can read it), the press, Cher-

---

[6] This entry was later adapted for *The Fall.*

agas,[7] etc. He sees the father begin to take shape. Then everything fades. Ultimately there is nothing.

It is always so on this earth, where there are 50, 70 years . . .[8]

At 40, Maillol[9] meets V. B., a Jewish Romanian painter who took refuge at Collioure in order to elude the Germans. He meets him in the street, recognizes the painter in him, invites him to come show him his pictures. The following day V.B. goes, is received with open arms, and explains his situation. "This house is yours," M. says, his only response. He provides a cup of coffee. He opens the carton while smiling at V.B. and finally looks at the first picture, distinctly surrealist: A woman who ends as a tree. Maillol bursts out: "No, no, not that, it's not possible. Out of here!"

Nietzsche. "They all talk about me. . . . But none *think* about me."

Le Pilori. "He must be blamed. It is necessary to blame his ugly manner of appearing honest and not being so." In the first person. Incapable of loving, he forces himself to, etc.

What the collaborationist left approves of, passes over in silence or considers inevitable; in no particular order:

1) The deportation of tens of thousands of Greek children.

---

[7] An Algerian village in the Sahel region.
[8] Illegible sequence.
[9] Aristide Maillol (1861–1944), French artist, who, like Camus, was killed as a passenger in a car accident.

2) The physical disposal of the Russian peasant class.

3) The millions of people in concentration camps.

4) The political abductions.

5) The near daily political executions behind the iron curtain.

6) Anti-Semitism.

7) Stupidity.

8) Cruelty.

The list is open. But this is enough for me.

Tolstoy's Journal. Three demons:

1) the play (possible struggle)

2) sensuality (very difficult struggle)

3) vanity (the most terrible of all).

"'I consider,' he says in a letter to his aunt, 'that without religion man can be neither good nor happy. . . . But I do not believe.'"

Id. "The truth is horrible."

October '53. Noble trade where one must, without budging, let oneself be insulted by a lackey of letters or of the party! In other times, which were said to be degrading, one at least retained the right to provoke without ridicule and to kill. Idiotic, for sure, but this made the insult less comfortable.

There are people whose religion consists of always forgiving offenses, but who never forget them. For me, I don't have what it takes to forgive the offense, but I always forget it.[1]

---

[1] A slightly altered version of this entry appears in *The Fall*.

Those who have been fertilized both by Dostoyevsky and Tolstoy, who understand both of them equally, with the same facility, these sorts are always formidable to themselves and to others.

October '53. Publication of Actuelles II.[2] The inventory is complete—the commentary and polemic. From now on, creation.

Shortly after great historical crises one finds oneself as dissatisfied and sick as on the morning following a night of excess. But there is no aspirin for the historical hangover.

These thoughts that you do not speak and that put you above all things, in a free and brisk air.

It is said that Nietzsche, after breaking with Lou, entered into a final solitude, walked at night in the mountains that dominate the Gulf of Genoa and lit immense fires there that he watched smolder. I've often thought of these fires and their gleam has danced behind my entire intellectual life. So even though I've sometimes been unjust toward certain thoughts and certain men whom I've met in this century, it is because I've unwillingly put them in front of these fires and they were promptly reduced to ashes.

In a letter to Hawthorne, Melville speaks of Moby Dick: "Here is the book's secret epigraph: Ego non baptiso te in nominee . . ."

---

[2] Camus' *Actuelles I, II,* and *III* have never fully appeared in English, though selected essays from each volume were published in the collection *Resistance, Rebellion, and Death.*

Id. "When I was writing this book I was aware of an allegorical construction on which the entire book, as well as each one of its parts, rested."

Id. After having finished M.B. and having read Hawthorne's appreciative letter: "I experience a strange feeling of satisfaction and irresponsibility; no desire for debauchery."

And then "I feel that I will leave this world with less bitterness after having known you."

Cf. The theme of the story "The Happy Failure"[3]: praise God for this failure.

Nietzsche. One could classify religious men as top-notch artists.

Nietzsche: *Dawn.* "Never keep silent, never conceal what one can think against your own thoughts. Swear it solemnly. It is the first act of loyalty that you owe to your thought."

Beyond . . . : "If one has character, one has in his life a characteristic experience that eternally recurs." Question then: to find the event and give it its name.

Genealogy . . . : "Whoever has ever built a new heaven has found the necessary power for this endeavor *only at the bottom of his own hell.*"

"Polyphony" of certain natures.

---

[3] Herman Melville, "The Happy Failure: A Story of the River Hudson."

Nietzsche (*Human, All Too Human*): "A little while after I fell ill, more than ill, tired by the continual disillusion caused by all that enthused us modern men . . ."

. . . "Here a man who speaks suffers and is deprived, but he expresses himself as if he did not suffer and did not deprive himself."

. . . "From now on solitary, I take the side against myself and everything that, in fact, opposed me and made me suffer."

Unique and gigantic goal: the recognition of truth.

Eternal recurrence: Exalt what is and adore that it returns. (Without metaphysics, it indeed remains only that.)

Note to Lou (1882). "In bed. Acute crisis. I despise life."

Necessity of an aristocracy. In the present, one can imagine only two of them: the one of intelligence and the one of work. But intelligence alone is not an aristocracy. Nor work (the examples, in both cases, are obvious). Aristocracy is not primarily the enjoyment of certain rights, but primarily the acceptance of certain duties that alone legitimize the rights. The aristocracy is asserting itself and at the same time stepping aside. To leave oneself (the definition of duty), intelligence cannot move toward privileges. Some take part of intelligence, others are the opposite of intelligence. And duty consists neither of asserting oneself nor of suppressing oneself but of making sure one serves what one claims. Thus, intelligence can move only toward the work that is its duty and its limit. Work, for its part, cannot move toward stultification, unconscious or conscious (generalized humiliation of intelligence), which is either itself or its opposite (see above). Thus, work can only move toward intelligence. Finally, in the present, the aristocracies of work and intelligence are not possible until they recognize one another and begin to walk one toward the other in order to one day establish a single superior image of man.

Obligation to hide a part of his life gave him the appearance of virtue.

The only source of aristocracy is the people. Between the two there's nothing. This nothing, which for 150 years has been the bourgeoisie, tries to give shape to the world and obtains nil, a chaos that survives only because of its past roots.

Walpole. "His good sense went as far as genius."

Utilize his vices, be wary of his virtues.

Brupbacher.[4] "Nobody should produce more philanthropy nor morality than he naturally secretes." He thought that the mission of the militant philosopher consisted of supporting all factors of freedom in all classes.

W. Whitman. "When liberty goes out of a place, it is not the first thing to go. It waits for all the rest to go, it is the very last."

Van Gogh, stuck with a common woman, Christine, then abandoned her when she was in the maternity ward. Gau-

---

[4] Fritz Brupbacher (1874–1945), Swiss physician and writer, author of *Socialisme et liberté* (*Socialism and Liberty*).

guin, waking in the night, saw Van Gogh leaning over him and looking at him fixedly. At the Saint-Rémy asylum, the count of G. beats his chest with a piece of wood while repeating: "my mistress, my mistress!"

Salacrou,[5] in the notes that accompany his Theatre, Volume VI, recounts the following story: "A little girl about to turn 10 declares: 'When I grow up, I'll register with the cruelest party.' Questioned, she explains: 'If my party is in power, I'll have nothing to fear and if it is the other, I'll suffer less since the party which will persecute me will be the less cruel one.'" I don't much believe in this little girl's story. But I know this reasoning very well. It's the shameful, but effective reasoning of 1954's French intellectuals.

Dostoyevsky's father made him whip both the peasants who bowed to him and those who did not bow to him. In both cases they appeared, according to him, audacious.[6] After the wife whom he tormented dies, he gets drunk at night and talks to her, taking in turn a woman's voice and then a man's voice. He is murdered. Head shattered, genitals crushed between two stones. Two months later, D., who hated his father, sees an interment, collapses, and groans.

Id. Spechniov (the petrashevskist[7]—"The man of irony, of liberty, and of power") and "each one is guilty of all, for all." Etym. root of Stavrogin: *stauros*: the cross.

---

[5] Armand Salacrou (1899–1989), French playwright.

[6] These lines were later adapted for *The Fall*.

[7] Petrashevsky was the organizer of an intellectual circle where people discussed revolutionary ideas. Dostoyevsky and his brother Michel began attending in 1847. Inside this circle, Nicolas Spechniov brought to life a more radical tendency. He was one of the models for Stavrogin. During the night of April 22–23, 1849, Dostoyevsky and thirty-three members of Petrashevsky's circle were arrested.

The Russian's hatred for the form that limits. They have pushed the revolution to its end. Berdyaev[8] notes somewhere that they have never had a Renaissance. Anxiety, always, Id. According to Berdyaev, the absence of chivalry has had disastrous consequences for the Russian moral culture.

Carlyle, Nietzsche, Dostoyevsky, are they revolutionaries? They are called counterrevolutionaries, though.

Adaptation of The Possessed.
Cf. Berdyaev. "Shatov, Verkhovensky, Kirilov, these are the many disaggregated fragments of Stavrogin's personality, emanations of this extraordinary personality that becomes exhausted as it dissipates. The enigma of Stavrogin, the secret of Stavrogin, such is the unique theme of The Possessed."

Dostoyevsky's Thesis: The same paths that lead the individual to crime lead the society to revolution.
Verkhovensky: "The most important force of the revolution is the shame of having one's own opinion."
Cf. Guardini,[9] pp. 40–41 and 202.

A priest who regrets having to leave his books when dying? Which proves that the intense pleasure of eternal life does not infinitely exceed the gentle company of books.

---

[8] Nikolai Berdyaev (1874–1948), Russian philosopher, who worked with both political and religious subject matter.
[9] Romano Guardini (1885–1968), priest and writer, wrote *L'Univers religieux de Dostoievski* (*The Religious Universe of Dostoyevsky*).

May 8. Fall of Dien Bien Phu. As in '40, mixed feelings of shame and rage.

The evening of the massacre, the result is clear. Right-wing politicians have placed the unfortunate ones in an indefensible situation and, at the same time, the leftists shoot them in the back.

According to Johnson (Boswell)[1] the perfect courtesy consists of not carrying the imprint of any profession whatsoever, but on the contrary, having a general ease in all manners and in all circumstances.

Id. Remarrying: "The triumph of hope over experience."

Id. J.'s friend: "I have tried, in my time, to be a philosopher but I do not know why, I was always interrupted by cheerfulness."

Id. "When we are reunited for some time, you will see that my brother is quite entertaining.

– I will be waiting, Sir, J. says."

Socrates learned to dance at an advanced age.

Johnson: "No man is a hypocrite in his pleasures."[2]

Before dying he thinks a "curious thought": we do not receive letters in our grave.

Don Juan Faust[3]
1) To be right
2) Nothing is allowed

---

[1] James Boswell's *Vie de Samuel Johnson* (*Life of Samuel Johnson*) was published in France in 1954.

[2] Camus adapted this quote into *The Fall*: "No man is a hypocrite in his pleasures; have I read that or did I think it, my dear compatriot?"

[3] Outline for a play that would have blended the character from the myth of Don Juan with that of Faust.

3) He consents to the stratagem of the Franciscans who kill him.[4]

Aix-en-Provence? Romanticism?

Sgnarelle[5] would be M. Nothingness from l'Impromptu des Philosophes.[6] It is he who announces "He will not come" (he reprimands Doña Anna's father who interrogates Don Juan about his vices. See Impromptu).

Don Juan is Faust without the pact—(develop).

Act III, in Brazil with the slaves. Act IV, Act V becomes man and solitary. *Solitary with all.*

D.J. Pact with the devil but without the devil. *To bet for the world*, the sensation and the pleasure, is to make a pact with the devil. *To bet for justice* is also to make a pact.

At the request of Massignon, I write to the President of the Republic to request pardon for those condemned to death at Moknine.[7] A few days later, I find a response in the newspaper: three of the condemned have been shot. *Fifteen days after the execution*, the director of the cabinet informs me that my letter "held the attention" of the President and was transmitted to the higher council of the magistracy. Bureaucracy of dreamers.

Two million union members out of eleven million employees. In 1947, there were seven million union members.

---

[4] See *Notebooks 1935–1942*: "For Don Juan. See Larousse: the Franciscan monks killed him and then presented him as if he had been struck down by the Commander."

[5] Ostensibly a reference to Molière's *Sgnarelle ou le cocu imaginaire* (*Sgnarelle: The Imaginary Cuckold*).

[6] *L'Impromptu des philosophes* (*The Philosopher's Farce*) stars M. Nothingness as its main character, an almost certain play on Sartre and his novel *Being and Nothingness*.

[7] In 1954, seven Tunisians were condemned to death for having killed three policemen. Camus' letter to President Coty was written April 12, 1954.

Play. A happy man. And nobody can put up with him.

In the water, the turtle becomes a bird. The large turtle of the warm seas glides within the tepid waters like a handsome albatross.

Atonal music, music for the voices, for the feverish voice of modern man.

Letter to M. "Do not curse the West. For me, I cursed it at the time of its splendor. But today, while it succumbs under the weight of its faults and its long-past glory, I will not add to its weight. . . . Do not envy those of the East, the sacrifice of intelligence and of heart to the gods of history. History has no gods, and intelligence, enlightened by the heart, is the only god, under a thousand forms, who has ever been saluted in this world."

Chekhov: "It is not glory that is essential for the writer . . . it is the patience to endure." "To carry his cross and keep hope."

The School of Critics: the "laws" of the theatre.
– If I have understood well, Sir, I must follow with punctuality the laws that neither Aeschylus, nor Shakespeare, nor Calderon, nor Corneille, nor any of the other great dramatic geniuses could keep themselves from breaking.
– It would be more accurate to say that only Shakespeare, Aeschylus, and the others could allow themselves to break these laws.

– By taking your advice, though, I will be neither one of these great creators.

– Would you claim to be?

– To be, no. But to become. And if not, why write? I will fail, that is almost certain. But to have tried, it will give to my life a taste that you strip away from me in advance. And Shakespeare, after all, was born from a hundred pretentious and desperate fools who wanted to be Shakespeare. As for Feydeau, it could have only come from Feydeau (I laugh, note it well, but rarely beyond one act).

Play. Today, King Lear is a patrician dispossessed by the Socialists.

Id. A Caligula who no longer accuses the world, but himself.

Death of Marcel Herrand.[8]

Virtuous men often make the citizens pusillanimous. At the root of true courage, imbalance.

According to our existentialists, every man is responsible for what he is. What can possibly explain the total disappearance of compassion in their universe of pushy old men. Yet they claim to fight against social injustice. Then there are people who are not responsible for what

---

[8] Marcel Herrand (1897–1953) died of cancer just eight days before the opening of the Festival of Angers, which he was set to direct. Camus met with Herrand in Nice a few months before his passing and went on to direct the festival after his death (Herrand was nonetheless billed as the director).

they are; the cur is innocent of his misery. So? the disabled, the ugly, the timid. . . . And to conclude, compassion, again?

Pericles before the grave of a young man: "The year has lost its spring."

When they spoke of me as a "director" (somebody who, in short, showed good direction) a part of me, of course, swelled with idiotic vanity. But during all these years, another part of me has never ceased dying of shame.

M.H.[9] The terribly sad air of the dying—and the stubborn and provincial air of those who assist in the death throes. He, so urbane, and then all of a sudden almost encircled in this alcove, where only . . .

There are moments when letting yourself go to sincerity is equivalent to an inexcusable laxity.

The First Man: Stages of Jessica: the sensual girl. The young lover infatuated with the absolute. The true lover. Accomplishment regardless of ambiguous beginnings.
"When I loved her the most, someone inside of me hated her for what she had done, seen, and suffered. Especially suffered. I hated her for not having waited for me, dead, until the early morning hour. And I hated her in the presence

---

[9] Marcel Herrand.

of someone else inside of me who laughed at this ridiculous pretension."

Jonas.[1] There is a housing shortage. And then the paintings accumulate and take his place. Hence, the closet.

At the moment when he does nothing more – "He heard them running through the rooms . . . life, the noise that men make, how beautiful. The girl laughed. How he loved them! How he loved them!"

Play. The Liar.
1) He lies. Two women enter.
2) He tells the truth.
3) Facing catastrophe, he lies again. (She tears up the paper that would get her out of the lie.)

A play about the impossibility of solitude. *They are always there.*[2]

Novel. Best wishes (to my son who will start again).

What man accepts with the most difficulty is being judged. Hence, the attachment to the mother, or the blinded lover, or the love of animals as well.

---

[1] Notes for "The Artist at Work," one of the stories in *Exile and the Kingdom.*

[2] Similar to the theme of "The Artist at Work." In 1953, Camus wrote a "mimodrame," *La Vie d'artiste* (*Life of the Artist*), in which a painter is prevented from working by socialites, friends, and disciples.

Thermonuclear bomb: to some extent, generalized death coincides with the human condition on this point of view. It suffices then to settle oneself. We rediscover the first, and oldest, of problems. Arriving at infinity, we begin again at zero. 2nd displacement of the problem: the universal curse no longer has God as author, but men. Men have finally become equals with God, but only in his cruelty. We must therefore begin again the revolt of ancient times, but this time against humanity. We demand a new Satan to deny the power of men.

Bizarre. "Dirty kike," the elder says. And the little one hits him. He had to hit him. But he did not want to do it. He did not hate the head that he hit. . . . And the other one did not want to do it either. He did not want to call this likable little one a kike, did not want to hit him. But he had to respond and therefore he hit him.

Fantastic tales.

Christ-Pan.

Aesthetics. Sometimes when one moves away from emotion, the cry bursts forth. Other times, one moves to meet emotion, still alive in the memory, by a long turning of sentences and words that finally guide us there and, in fact, resuscitate the emotion, no longer like a cry, but rather like a large wave of which the magnitude. . . .

Id. If I say, "He has a nose like a pumpkin," that does not mean, "like a peach," does it? Thus, art is a calculated exaggeration.

Char and the lioness' love in the Jardin des Plantes. He puts his head through the bars. She rolls over. She opens her little paws. . . .

On all the paths of the world, millions of men have preceded us and their traces are visible. But on the oldest sea, our silence is always the first.

Nobody deserves to be loved—nobody measures up to that immeasurable gift. Those who receive love then discover injustice.

If I had not given in to my passions perhaps I would have had the tools to intervene in the world, to change something. But I have given in to them and this is why I am an artist, and this alone.

Somebody inside of me has always tried, with all his strength, to be nobody.

At the boundary of this long burning thought, far off in the distance, total acceptance.

At the very moment when after so much effort I laid down the limits, believing to be able to reconcile the irreconcilable, the limits burst and I was hurried into a silent unhappiness.

NOTEBOOK VIII

August 1954 – July 1958

8.15.1954

Mahler's 4th symphony in G major for sopranos and orchestra. At times, Mahler, by contrast, makes one appreciate Wagner, showing how much the latter remained master of his fog. Other times, Mahler is excellent.

8.16.1954

X. says to me: "Why don't we accept the idea of eternal life? Because it is, in the end, a private beatitude of consciousness—and we want to be, which is to say we want to know that we are. But then why reproach the world for precisely what gives us consciousness, which is to say pain and suffering (this is indeed the contradiction of modern atheism). Me, I have always accepted suffering with a sort of joy, the joy of being." I say to him that therein lies the genius. The genius? Yes, the genius of life, which she alone, among all the beings I have met, carries with natural pride.

17. *Berl.*[1]

It is easier for intellectuals to say no than to say yes. At the end of his life, looking at volumes of his work, Doctor Reclus, who sided with Dreyfus, realized that there were two years when he produced nothing. Ah! yes, Dreyfus: he devoted those two years to *studying* files of the affair. Today one takes a side based on a single reading of an article.[2]

Wasted afternoon.

18.

No way out of it. Suicide. Those who are already dead, what then do they expect? Cemetery of Anet where the ivy has split an old flagstone.

For many years I've lived cloistered in her love. Never having ceased to love her, today it is necessary that I flee, to at least have her concern, which is difficult.

19.

Terrible morning. Afternoon exhibition of Cézanne: the first mad and morbid paintings (sexual obsession in particular). A madness of this sort required the terrible discipline that Cézanne had. The demented alone are classic because

---

[1] Emmanuel Berl (1892–1976), French journalist, who had become friends with Camus.

[2] Alfred Dreyfus (1859–1935), French Jew at the center of the Dreyfus Affair, in which he was wrongfully convicted of treason. The affair's fallout created a divisive political scandal throughout France.

they are that or nothing. C. pushed demand to the limit of his disorder and chose still-life and landscape painting because he found in them an architecture, a geometry. Toward the end he returned to bodies and faces and rediscovered madness, the madness that he mastered. Here, Cubism is ordered (foretold).[3]

Mail.

20.

Mail. Dead day.

25.

Dead day. N.A. (Derain, crazy after hemiplegia, hit by an automobile. His wife and his former mistress[4] protect the paintings with official seals while he is delirious in a clinic.)

The Gate of Hell.[5] A Japanese film that feels a bit American. But next to this art, the barbarity of ours.

22.

Sad and wise nature of the Île-de-France.

23–24.

Dead days. Lunch with Berl.

25.

Work except in the morning. Museum of Man. I leave there with a mouth full of ashes, the osseous ashes of

[3] Questionable reading.
[4] Quite possibly Mado Anspach.
[5] *Jigoku-Mon (The Gate of Hell)*, a film by Kinugasa, which received the Grand Prix du Festival at Cannes in 1954.

skeletons and mummies. Peruvian mummy: [. . .][6] of history. Who was she?

Action and writing: they are not certain about being right, but this uncertainty gives them a guilty conscience. They write then to get rid of this guilty conscience. With this intention they will seek new arguments, which they will find, and then assert a little further. The opposition will do the same. Thus, the positions will stiffen. So many repeated assertions will be equivalent to actions. Will soon provoke them. Thus, the victorious party will have enough charges on the day of victory. By means of continually fleeing their guilty consciences, the losers will have found true guilt and will answer for it, never having wanted that. Another day, the victors, in turn, will be vanquished and will respond, never having wanted that. History is a long crime perpetrated by the innocent.

September 7.
The children return. Catherine cannot fall asleep as she is scared of dying (due to the pain in her chest). That this anxiety already tortures these small beings, is this not truly the final outrage?

September 8.
N.A. calls me: Derain just died. Paralyzed on one side, crazy, persecuted by his wife who put seals on his paintings. N.A. is desperate. Nothing to do. Poor Derain whose gruff intensity I loved. Too alive for his own life.

---

[6] Illegible word.

9.

For X. (and her family) love mixes with suffering, anguish. To love is to suffer from or for. For me, love has never been separate from a certain state of joyful innocence. Hardly had I experienced that when I was plunged into guilt and could no longer truly love.

20.

It's not dying that I fear, but living in death.

Annihilation is nothing to fear for those who have lived long.

God is not needed to create guilt or to punish. Human beings suffice.[7] He could, if worse comes to worst, establish innocence.

21.

How could he preach justice, he who has not even managed to make it reign over his own life?

In the night, the murderer undressed himself and with axe blows slaughtered his family.

M.: "You are secretive, kind, and (to compensate for what is repulsive in kindness) you are passionate and at times unfair."

October 5.[8]

Scenery in Rotterdam at night: all of its luminous carcasses raised above its canals.

---

[7] A slightly modified version of these lines appear in *The Fall*: "God is not needed to create, nor to punish. Our fellow humans suffice, aided by ourselves."

[8] In October 1954, Camus visited Holland. This is where *The Fall* is set. In the notebook entries for September 20 and 21, notes already begin to appear on guilt and justice, foretelling the book's appearance.

The Hague.

This entire world gathered in a small space of houses and waters, one silently stuck to another, and it rained at length over the entire city, without a moment to breathe, while ugly, sulky little children directed the traffic of placid cars and beautiful [. . .][9] railings of the royal museum to wash the pediment's opulent decorations while it was still raining and a pianist on a tricycle [. . .][1] played Chopin's Tristesse accompanied by a [. . .][2] violinist and a distinguished beggar who collected kindly donated copper coins, meager offerings that made a soft sound and that were meant for the grimacing gods of Indonesia whom one sees in the windows and who wander invisible in the air of Holland, manning the dispossessed colonist's nostalgia. O Java, distant island whose sons serve coffee here while it still rains and where in the wet air hangs the marvelous memory of the girl at the door of inexhaustible beginnings, the tubercular light and silence of Rembrandt's old brother whose eyes look without desire at the eternal country.

October 6.

It rains for days and the cold wind [. . .].[3] That was over there in Rotterdam, all freshly nickel-plated, and Amsterdam always wet; and here in The Hague perched on bicycles with high handlebars, like funeral swans circling the cold Vigver, between the live eels of the fish market and the marvelous jewels of unattractive windows, the same color as the dead leaves stuck all over the ground and the smoked herrings, which, for a long time, swam in the old gold seas.

[9] Three illegible words.
[1] One illegible word.
[2] One illegible word.
[3] Four illegible words.

O Cipango, over there and here [. . .][4] Holland, mild-mannered Holland, where one learns the patience[5] to die.

Conversion to the serious. Seriousness is an accepted lie and recognized infirmity. For all the rest, quiet sincerity.

Don Juan.[6]
She: I always knew that you didn't love me.
But I loved you.
You spoke to me and occasionally looked at me over my head.
He: I don't seduce, I adapt.

October 26.
The opposite of reaction is not revolution, but creation. The world is in an unending state of reaction and thus unendingly in danger of revolution. What defines progress, if it is such, is that without compromise, creators of all kinds triumph over the mind, over reaction, and over inactivity without revolution being necessary. When there are no more of these creators, revolution is inevitable.

According to Koestler, old Turkish law considered a crime committed by [. . .][7] an extenuating circumstance.

---

[4] One illegible word.
[5] Questionable reading.
[6] The topic of Don Juan always haunted Camus. In 1937, in Algiers, he assembled and acted in Pushkin's *Don Juan* with the Théâtre du Travail. Notes on Don Juan can be found in the 1940s notebooks. In Notebook VII, on pages 95–96, the blending of the myths of Don Juan and Faust foretells the planned project *Don Faust*.
[7] Two illegible words.

Honeysuckle—for me, its scent is tied to Algiers. It floated in the streets that led toward the high gardens where the girls awaited us. Vines, youth . . .

The white rose of morning carries the scent of pepper and water.

Julia.[8]
Last act: J. I am ugly.
d'Al yes.

Everything, in me and in people, draws me downward.

November 1st.
I often read that I am atheistic; I hear people speak of my atheism. Yet these words say nothing to me; for me they have no meaning. I do not believe in God *and* I am not an atheist.

As a creator I have given life to death itself. That is all that I had to do before dying.

Pavese: "We are idiots. The little bit of freedom that the government leaves us, we allow it to be gobbled up by women."

---

[8] Plan for a play about Julie de Lespinasse. These two retorts are exchanged between Julie and d'Alembert. See Notebook VII, pages 54–55.

Rembrandt: glory until 1642, at 36 years of age. From this date on, the march of solitude and poverty. An infrequent experience and more significant than the banal one of the ignored artist. About such an experience, nothing has been said.

B.C.: "Nature does not give this spiritual force to man so that he can enjoy it for himself. She entrusts it to him for a use beyond his person."

Id.: "An authentic creator is organically subjected to the law of pleasure."

Spengler says that the soul of Russia is a revolt against Antiquity. True enough. See Berdyaev also: Russia never had the Renaissance.

Text about Hébertot.[9] In the middle of the grotto is a large white sperm whale. Between his teeth he filters everything, allowing only the plankton of tasty authors to reach him.

Realism. Everybody is realistic. Nobody is. Finally, it is not aesthetics that matter but personal demeanor.

The literature of totalitarian countries does not die so much because it is controlled as because it is cut off from

---

[9] Director of the theatre that bore his name and that staged *Caligula* in 1945 and *The Just* in 1949.

other literatures. Any artist who, from the beginning, is not open to the whole of reality is incomplete.

November 7, 1954.
   41 years old.

The Bacchae.[1]
   In Sicily. Now. A small village in the Palermo region. And everything has the same pleasantness.
   Very important works in view. In any case, there remains something of it. Ex: Don Juan, Faust, they're all part of it.[2]

Correct *The Rebel*, p. 225, 6th line (workmen instead of monks) and p. 229, 1st line.

Duperray[3] letter. "The revolutionary trade-unionists continue to devote themselves to their essential activity: searching for reasons to separate over common principles."

New title: A Puritan of Our Time.[4]

November 24. 10:00.
   Arrival in Turin this morning.[5] For several days, joy at the thought of rediscovering Italy. I have not seen it since my last

---

[1] Play by Euripides (406 B.C.). Camus seems to think about an adaptation (see pages 36–38).

[2] See notebook VII, pages 86–87, and Notebook VIII, page 111.

[3] Jean Duperray, militant trade-unionist and writer, acquaintance of Simone Weil in the 1930s. Author of *Harengs frits au sang* (*Fried Herring with Blood*).

[4] One of the many titles Camus was considering for what finally became *The Fall*.

[5] Camus traveled to Italy on the invitation of the Italian Cultural Association, for lectures in Turin, Genoa, and Rome.

stay in 1938. The war, the resistance, Combat, and all these years of revolting seriousness. Travels, but instructive and where the heart falls silent. It seemed to me that my youth, a renewed strength, and a lost light awaited me in Italy. Also, I was going to flee this universe (my home), which for a year now has destroyed me cell by cell; perhaps this escape would save me forever. Actually, yesterday when the train started moving, I was no happier. Tired at first, and then there was the meeting with Grenier where I wished we could have spoken freely, but we could not; even X. could not help me to leave contented. During the night, however, between brief slumbers, a happiness came, yet still remote.

At 7 o' clock this morning, the realization that we are in Italy. I shake myself and open the blind: a landscape covered in snow and fog. It is snowing over all of northern Italy. Alone in my compartment, a laughing fit took hold of me. It is not cold. Yet I.A., who waits for me at the train station, claims she is freezing to death. With her pretty, wavering French and her small, calm, gracious gestures (she reminds me of Maman), blushed from the cold like a little snow flower, she returns a little bit of Italy to me. Already the Italians on the train, and soon those of the hotel as well, have warmed my heart. People whom I have always liked and who make me feel my exile in the French people's perpetual bad mood.

From my hotel room I can see the snow continue to fall over Turin. Still I laugh at my disillusion. But courage returns to me.

Turin beneath the snow and fog. At the Egyptian gallery, the mummies, which have been pulled from the sand without wrappings, shrivel from the cold. I like the grand streets, paved and well spaced. This city is built as much of space as of walls. I am going to see the house at 6 Piazza Carlo Alberto, where Nietzsche worked before plunging into madness. I have never been able to read the account of Overbeck's arrival without crying: his entrance into the room where Nietzsche, insane now, raves, and then crying, throws himself into Overbeck's arms. In front of the house I tried to think of he whom I have always loved with as much affection as admiration, but it was in vain. I find him better in the city—which I understand he loved, despite the low sky—and I understand why he loved it.

Short Story. The camp prisoners elect a pope, choosing from those among them who have suffered most, denying the other—the Roman—who lives in the luxurious Vatican. They call theirs *Father* even though he is one of the youngest there, they obey him in all, and will die for him until he himself dies defending his sons (or better yet he refuses to die and protects himself because he has others to defend and this is the beginning).[6]

November 25.

Grey misty day. I wander in Turin. Crowned skulls on the hill. Downtown, at the heart of an immense view, bronze horses rise up in the fog. Turin, a city of horses frozen in the same élan in the place where Nietzsche became insane, stopped a horse from being beaten by its driver, and then madly embraced its muzzle. Dinner—villa Camerana.

November 26.

Long walk in the hills of Turin. In the surrounding sky, the snowy Alps appear and disappear in the fog. The air is

---

[6] An idea used in *The Fall*. Clamence recounts that when he was held captive in Tripoli, Libya, his fellow captives elected him pope.

fresh, humid, and smells like autumn. The city below is covered in fog. Far from everything, tired, and strangely happy. Evening, lecture.

November 27.

Depart for Genoa in the morning with I.A.; strange little being, clean, rich in heart and will, with a sort of reflective renouncement that seems surprising for such a young person. She wants to "laugh and regret." In the case of religion, she believes in "detached love." Obviously many aspects of Maman, whom I dream of with sadness. I always have this grave, unbelievable death on my heart. . . .

Rain and fog all over Piedmont and Liguria. In the middle of the snowfields, we cross the mountains bordering the Ligurian coast. Four tunnels later and the snow disappears whereas the rain redoubles on the slopes descending toward the sea. Two hours after arrival, a lecture. Dinner at the Palais Doria. The old marquise appears emaciated, everything except her eyes and heart. As I leave, I walk in a Genoa finally rediscovered, washed by voluminous waters. Black and white marbles shine, lights fuse in the streets, large arteries, banal.

From the VIth century to the year 1800, the population of Europe never exceeded 180 million.

From 1800 to 1914, the population went from 180 million to 460 million!

Ortega y Gasset.[7] Who wants to know to whom he speaks—to write—

---

[7] José Ortega y Gasset (1883–1955), Spanish philosopher.

Distinguishes society from association.

Freedom and pluralism are the two dominant components in Europe.

Philosopher and philosophy professor, see p. 26—on the true aristocracy: passion.

Humboldt.[8] In order for the human being to enrich and perfect himself, a variety of positions are necessary. Maintenance of this variety is the central effort of true liberalism.

Today's Russia sees the triumph of individualism in its cynical form.

Ortega y Gasset. History: the eternal struggle between paralytics and epileptics.

Every society is based on aristocracy, because this one, the true one, is demanding with regard to itself, and without this demand every society would die.

Ortega y Gasset. The creative life supposes a regimen of elevated hygiene, great nobility, and constant stimuli, which excite the conscience, and more, the creative life is an energetic life.

How the alleys teem with shadows. Content and fatigued.

---

[8] Wilhelm von Humboldt (1767–1835), philologist and German politician.

November 28.

Long walk in Genoa. A fascinating city and quite similar to the one I remembered.[9] Superb monuments erupt in a tight corset of small streets crawling with life. Beauty is made on the spot here, radiating in the life of everyday. A singer on the corner of the street improvises the scandals of current events. A singing newspaper.

The small cloister of San Matteo. The wind drives the rain in bursts across the large leaves of medlar trees. Brief instant of happiness. Life must now be changed.

Evening: departure for Milan, in the rain. Arrived in the rain. What Stendhal loved here is quite dead.

November 29.

Last Supper[1] – Vinci is definitely at the beginning of the Italian decline. Cloister of San Ambrogio. Lecture. In the evening I travel by train to Rome, exasperated by the stupid society life that follows the lectures. Incapable of putting up with more than half an hour of these antics. Sleepless night.

30.

Finally, in the morning, pale but determined sunshine over the Roman countryside. Stupidly, tears come to my eyes. Rome. Another one of these luxurious hotels, stupid like the society that maintains them. I'll move tomorrow. With N., I look at the Birth of Venus. Walk along the villas Borghese and Pincio: everything is painted on the sky with a brush of rare bristles. I sleep. Last lecture. Free at last.

---

[9] Camus had previously visited Genoa in September 1937.
[1] Leonardo da Vinci's *The Last Supper* is located in the dining hall at Santa Maria delle Grazie in Milan, Italy.

Dinner with N., Silone,[2] and Carlo Levi.[3] Tomorrow will be good.

December 1st to the 3rd.

There are cities like Florence, small Tuscan or Spanish cities, which carry the traveler, support his every step, and render those steps lighter. Others, like New York, weigh on his shoulders and crush him such that he must learn little by little to stand up and to see.

This is how Rome weighs, but with a sensitive and light weight: one carries it on the heart like a corpus of fountains, gardens, and cupolas, one breathes beneath it, a little oppressed but strangely happy. This is a relatively small city, but from an aerial perspective it occasionally breaks out at the turning of a street, this sensitive and limited space breathes together with the traveler and lives with him.

Left the hotel for lodgings on the Villa Borghese. I have a balcony that extends over the gardens, and the view I found there warms my heart every time I see it. After so many years of a city without light, of rising in the fog, among the walls, I am ceaselessly nourished by this sky and these lines of trees that extend from Porta Pinciana to Trinità dei Monti and behind which Rome rolls out its cupolas and disorder.

Each morning when I go out on this balcony, still a little drunk with sleep, the birds' song surprises me, comes to find me at the bottom of my slumber, and comes to touch a

[2] Ignazio Silone (1900–1978), Italian novelist and socialist militant. In 1939, Camus wrote of his novel *Le Pain et le vin* (*Bread and Wine*) in *Alger-Républicain*. They met for the first time in 1948. From 1953 to 1957, Camus and Silone both collaborated with *Témoins*, a small revue of libertarian thought.

[3] Carlo Levi (1902–1976), Italian painter and writer, author of *Christ s'est arrêté à Eboli* (*Christ Stopped at Eboli*).

precise place that in a single stroke releases a sort of mysterious joy. For two days the weather has been nice and the beautiful December light before me outlines the curled-up cypresses and pines.

Here I regret the dark and derisory years I have lived in Paris. There is a reason of heart that I no longer want because it is useful to no one and puts me a hair's breadth from my own loss.

The day before yesterday, on the Forum—in the part that is badly ruined (close to the Coliseum), not in this extravagant flea market of pretentious columns found under Campidoglio—then on the admirable Palatine Hill where nothing exhausts the silence, the peace, the world always emerging and always perfect, I began to rediscover myself. It is this that the great images of the past serve, when nature can accommodate them and extinguish the sound that lies dormant in them, to gather the hearts and forces that will then better serve the present and the future. It is felt on the Via Appia where, even though I arrived at the end of the afternoon, I felt inside of me, while I was walking, a heart so full that life could have left me then. But I knew that it would continue, that there is a force in me that moves forward, and that this stopover would yet serve progress. (One year I did not work, I could not work even though ten topics were waiting, which I know were exceptional and I still could not tackle. About a year since, and I have not gone insane.) One could live well in this cloister, this room where Tasso[4] died.

Places in Rome. Piazza Navona. Sant' Ignazio and the others. They are yellow. The fountain basins are a little pink beneath the baroque gushing of water and stones. When one has beheld all, or beheld in any case all that one

---

[4] Torquato Tasso (1544–1595), Italian poet, who in his later years seemed to suffer a form of schizophrenia.

could behold, strolling without seeking *knowledge* is a perfect happiness.

Yesterday, during the night, in front of San Pietro in Montorio, Rome, beneath its fires, was like a harbor whose restlessness and noise had come to die at the foot of this silent embankment where we were.

It's a strange and insufferable certainty to know that monumental beauty always supposes servitude, that, however, servitude is beauty and one cannot help but desire beauty and one cannot desire servitude; servitude remains no less intolerable. Perhaps it's for this that I put the beauty of a landscape above all else—it's not paid for by any injustice and my heart is free there.

December 3.

Superb morning in the Villa Borghese. The light of Algerian mornings flows between fine pine needles and carves them out one by one. And in the Gallery,[5] full with a fair-blond light, Bernini amuses me, gorgeous and disconcerting when grace triumphs, as it does in the highly surrealist Apollo and Daphne (as an art, surrealism was initially a counteroffensive to the baroque), hideous when grace disappears, as in the disconcerting Truth Unveiled by Time. A vibrant painter also (Portraits).

Correggio's Danae, and especially Venus Blindfolding Cupid, by Titian, painted at age 90 and of timeless youth.

The Caravaggios, not those in St. Louis of the French,[6] seen in the afternoon, definitely superb with the contrast of

---

[5] The Borghese Gallery in Rome.
[6] The national French church of Rome, located in the heart of the city. Caravaggio was commissioned to produce paintings for the church's interior.

the violence and the mute layer of light. *Before Rembrandt.* Especially The Calling of St. Matthew: superb. C.[7] points out to me the constancy of the themes of youth and maturity. Moravia[8] had already spoken to me of the type of man Caravaggio had been: he committed several crimes, was robbed fleeing Tuscany, and then was thrown on a beach where he died, insane (1573–1610). Moravia also told me the true story of Cenci,[9] on whom he wants to base a play. Beatrice is buried beneath the altar of St. Louis of the French. Riots in Rome, the French Revolution. A French sans-culotte painter takes part in sacking St. Louis of the French. The tombs are opened. Beatrice's skeleton is there, the skull split, resting in the center of the body. The painter takes the skull and leaves, playing with it like a ball. This is the last image related to the terrible story of Beatrice Cenci.

At the end of the afternoon, I return to Janiculum. San Pietro in Montorio. Yes, this hill is my favorite place in Rome. High in the tender sky, groups of starlings, light as smoke, turn in all directions, crossing each other, scattering, and then gathering to plunge over the pines, which they graze before returning to the sky. When we go back down with N., we find them exhausted in the trees, the plane trees of Trastevere's Viale del Re, their numbers so enormous that each tree hums and crackles, covered with more birds than leaves. When evening falls, a deafening chirping covers the noises of this populated neighborhood, merges with the sputtering trolleys, and keeps all of the laughing heads turned up toward these enormous swarms of leaves and feathers.

[7] Likely Nicola Chiaromonte (1905–1972), Italian author and friend of Camus'.

[8] Alberto Moravia (1907–1990), famed Italian novelist, whose books were often adapted to the screen by cinematic luminaries such as Godard and Bertolucci.

[9] Beatrice Cenci (1577–1599) was at the center of a scandalous murder trial in Italy. She was eventually, alongside most of her family, beheaded.

The large brown Roman with the gentle and noble face, with a demeanor so simple and so proud, takes care of me at the lodging house. Short story. Love with the painter. And all the nobility on his side.

Write a BAROQUE text about Rome.

December 4.

Morning. Barberini Palace. Caravaggio's Narcissus, and especially this Madonna attributed to P. della Francesca, appears to me to belong rather to the wispier manner of Signorelli. Admirable in any case.

Lunch with Moravia and N. at Tivoli, and a long afternoon in Hadrian's Villa, the perfect location. Superb day, it's true, free of clouds and with a round sky whose sections disperse an even amount of light on the magnificent cypresses and the tall pines of the villa. Its sections of tall, ruined wall receive this even light on their honeycomb sheathing and in turn let escape secretions of honeyed light from their cement hives. Here, I can better see the difference between Roman light and others, that of Florence for example, more diffuse, silvery, spiritual, in short. Rome's light, on the contrary, is round, gleaming, and supple. It makes one think of bodies, with the opulence of felicitous flesh, the successful life. Backgrounds even more succulent. Birdsong among the ruins. In the face of this curious and happy perfection, the feeling that all is said.

Dinner, Piovene.[1] At the conclusion of thirty conversations, I begin to get an idea of the true situation here. Not of opinions but of factions. Few liberals, misery, its purpose, and little by little a certain inertia.

[1] Guido Piovene (1907–1974), Italian writer and friend of Camus'.

At forty years of age, one no longer complains of the bad, one recognizes it and struggles according to what one owes. One can then occupy oneself with creating without forgetting anything.

In The Last Judgment's movement of ascension, on the right side of the altar, Michelangelo's bodies had to be heavily muscled in order to give the impression of irresistible lightness. Light yet heavy. This is the intricacy of art.

In the Borgia apartments, Pinturicchio's Rhetoric carries a sword.

One's heart aches a little at the thought that Julius II destroyed Piero della Francesca's (and others) frescoes so that Raphael could paint his chambers; what have they paid for the superb Liberation of St. Peter?

Caravaggio's Deposition from the Cross. The Cross is not seen; definitely an exceptional painter.

December 6.
Grey day. Fever. I keep the room. Saw Moravia in the evening.

Novel.
The First Man repeats the entire journey in order to discover his secret: he is not the first. Every man is the first man, nobody is. This is why he throws himself at his mother's feet.

December 7.

Departing with Nicola and Francesco. The Roman countryside. F. is so beautiful and so removed from everything without ceasing to be present and human. The village of Circe.[2] Arrival in Naples. Lunch in Pozzuoli at a restaurant that is Padovani's twin. It is pouring rain in Naples, which increases my fever. In the evening the sky clears.

December 8.

I awaken with a serious fever. Last night I could not finish these notes. Despite that, a long walk in the "Barrios" behind the rue Santa Lucia. These are the slums behind the Champs-Élysées. The door is open and one sees three children in the same bed, occasionally with their father, not at all embarrassed to let themselves be exposed. All of this flapping linen gives Naples an air of perpetual festivity that comes, after all, from what the linen lacks and from the need to wash it day after day. These are the flags of misery. N.F. tonight. Then we leave in a damp carriage that smells of leather and dung. The friendships of men always taste good. N. takes us to a neighborhood in Porta Capuana. Main street climbs upward. On every balcony lamps are posed with their lampshades, and this gives to that misery an extraordinarily festive air. There is a kind of procession in front of the church. Flags wave above the packed crowd that tramples in the thick mud of cabbage debris left by the morning market. And especially the firecrackers in all the saints' behinds; the Virgin announces herself by backfiring. In one window, a demented person, eyes fixed, ignites dozens of firecrackers with the same mechanical gesture— one after the other—which he then hurls into the crowd and

---

[2] Homer, Virgil, Strabo, and Pliny mention Mount Circeo, in the south of Lake Sabaudia, under the name Circe Island. The village at the base is also called Circeo.

around which the children dance in a ring, like the Sioux, until they explode. The hostelry of the poor. They have outdone themselves. This is the Escurial of misery.

December 8.

In bed all day with a fever that won't let up. Ultimately I will not be able to go to Paestum. Return to Rome at the first sign of improvement, then Paris, that's all. There's something between the Greek temples and me: at the last moment something always intervenes that prevents me from going to them.[3]

Incidentally, this time there is no mystery. This exhausting year has brought me to my knees. The hope of recovering my strength and returning to work was purely sentimental. Instead of running toward a light that I can barely taste, I would do better, after all, to spend a year rebuilding my health and willpower. But for that I would have to free myself a little from all that weighs down on me. Those are the thoughts of bed and fever and of a traveler cloistered with Naples surrounding him. But they are true thoughts. Fortunately, I see the sea from my bed.

F.'s painter friend, extremely ignorant and having to illustrate the Passion of St. Matthew for a radio program, makes a saint surrounded by pretty women and mocking angels.

December 9.

Upon waking, the fever has disappeared. But stiff in the joints and punch-drunk. However, I decide to go (as every time, I draw energy from recognizing worse situations: prisoners, etc.). We leave in a beautiful sunshine. Sorrento (and

---

[3] In the summer of 1939, Camus had planned a trip to Greece, but the war intervened. He didn't travel to Greece for the first time until April 1955.

the delectable Cocumella garden), Amalfi a little too decorative where we lunch, then I drive to relieve F. who is tired, and the sun sets when, after having crossed an industrial region and then a curious ground that makes me think of Limbo (large reeds, skeletal and bare), we arrive at Paestum. Here the heart falls silent.

(Later.) At the end of the afternoon, I want to try to relive this arrival. We are welcomed at an inn close to the ruins by a nice old room with three beds and enormous bleached walls, rustic but of unquestionable cleanliness. A dog sticks close to me. The sun sets as, the gates being closed, we climb the ramparts to enter the field of ruins. Light still comes from the quite close blue sea, but the hills that face the sea are already black. When we arrive before the temple of Poseidon the already sleeping crows rise up in an extraordinary tumult of wings and cries, then fly around the temple, fall to the four corners and set out again like a salute to the admirable being of stone, nonetheless alive and unforgettable, appearing before our eyes. The hour, the black flight of crows, the birds' rare songs, the space between the sea and the hills, and one retains these exact and warm wonders; all of this in my fatigue and emotion puts me a hair's breadth away from tears. Then the interminable rapture, when everything falls silent.

Evening, silence, crows, like the birds of Lourmarin and the cat, my tears, music.

In the morning, in Tipasa, there is dew on the ruins. The world's youngest freshness on what is most ancient. Therein lies my faith and, in my opinion, the principle of art and life.

December 10.

Last night, walk toward the beach, among the reeds, ramparts, and buffaloes. The immense and muted sound of the sea, which intensifies little by little. The beach, tepid water under the night's grey and luminous sky. On the way back it rains a little and the sound of the sea dies down behind us. The buffaloes move gently, lowering their heads, still as the night. Gentleness.

I fall asleep after having gazed through my window at the temples in the night. The room with the thick and naked walls that I like so much is freezing cold. Cold all night. I open my windows; it is raining on the ruins. An hour later, at the time we are to leave, the sky is blue, the light fresh and magnificent. Endless amazement before this temple of enormous sponge pink columns, golden cork, its ethereal impression, its inexhaustible presence. Other birds have mixed with the crows but the latter still cover the temple with a black veil flapping in all directions, emitting raucous cries. The fresh smell of the small heliotropes, which cover the temple's surroundings.

Noises: the sound of water, dogs, a distant Vespa.

It is not the melancholy of ruined things that breaks the heart, but the desperate love of what lasts eternally in eternal youth: love of the future.

Still in the ruins between the hills and the sea. Difficult to pull myself away from these places, the first since Tipasa where I have known an abandonment of all being.

December 10.

Follow-up. We leave, nevertheless, and a few hours later, Pompeii. Interested of course, but never touched. The Romans are sometimes refined, never civilized. Lawyers and soldiers whom we confuse, God knows why, with the Greeks. They are the first, the true burglars of the Greek mind. Alas, conquered Greece did not conquer them in turn. Even though they borrowed the themes and forms of the grand art, they never understood the cold approximations that they would have been better off not making, such that the Greek naiveté and splendor would have appeared to us without intermediary. Compared with Hera of Paestum's temple, all the antiquity that covers Rome and Italy shatters to pieces and with it a comedy of false grandeur. By instinct, my heart has always known this, my heart which has never beaten for a single Latin poem (not even Virgil is admired, nor loved) and which has always ached for the flash of a tragic stanza or lyric hailing from Greece.

Returning to this precious Buchenwald that is Pompeii, the taste of ash and fatigue grows. We drive, alternating with F., and at 9:00 P.M. I arrive in Rome exhausted.

December 11.

Almost the entire day in bed. Continuous state of fever makes everything taste bland to me. Regain health at all cost. I need my strength. I do not need life to be easy for me but I want to be able to match myself up to it if it is difficult, being in command of whether I want to go where I am going. Will leave Tuesday.

December 12

A newspaper falls into my hands. The Parisian comedy that I had forgotten. The joke of Goncourt. This time, The Mandarins.[4] It appears that I am the hero. In fact, the author has taken a situation (the director of a newspaper originally from the Resistance) and all the rest is false: thoughts, feelings, and actions. Better: the questionable acts of Sartre's

---

[4] Simone de Beauvoir's novel, which won the Goncourt Prize in 1954.

life are liberally heaped on my back. Garbage anyway. But not intentionally, just sort of as one breathes.

Improved state. Grey day. It rains on Rome whose well-washed cupolas sparkle slightly. Lunch at F.G. Evening, alone, fever past.

December 13.

More Caravaggio. Santa Maria del Popolo. Rome's sadness is also with its streets, which are too high and too tight. This is why places there are so beautiful: they deliver; the baroque then triumphs over the Roman. Like its Roman couples frozen in stone who have nothing in common except that they stand very straight. The twilight hour that slips into the palace and collapses the proud façade. In the evening M. talks to me about Brancati[5] and his death. Dinner alone.

December 14. Departure.

Existentialism. When they accuse themselves one can be sure that it is always to crush others. Judge-penitents.[6]

With Luke true treason begins, causing the disappearance of Jesus' desperate dying cries.

M., to whom I say that there are certain roles that ask of the actor only virtuosity and in which the actor can experience his métier and his mastery, tells me that this does not interest her, that she does not like to play characters she cannot marry and live and feel herself then living another life through. And she concludes: "I like to perform because I am romantic."

[5] Vitaliano Brancati (1907–1954), Sicilian novelist.
[6] This is the first appearance of the "judge-penitent" concept, which would form the center of *The Fall*.

Morals. Not to take what one does not desire (difficult).[7]

I have always hoped to become better. I have always decided to do whatever is necessary to this end. Whether I have actually done it is another question.

For me, was marriage not a more civilized sensual adventure? It was that.

If I bloom, she wilts. She cannot live without leaning on my blossom. Thus, we are two opposing poles of psychology.

The opposite of the subterranean man: the man without resentment. But the catastrophe is the same.

This world wiggles quite a bit because, like a cut worm, it has lost its head. It searches for its aristocrats.

La Martinière, the white boat that transported the prisoners to Cayenne—and made a stopover in Algiers to load new cargo on board (my reportage[8] on a day of pouring rain—the boat covered with shaven convicts—the interior, two cages, etc. – The same trip that I made but in a comfortable cabin) – A story?

The First Man. Ambition made him laugh. He did not want to have, he did not want to possess, he wanted to be. For that only obstinacy.

From the moment the private life is thrown on display, explained to so many people, it becomes the public life, and it is vain to hope to maintain it.

---

[7] See *The Fall*: ". . . one day you find yourself in the position of taking without really desiring. Believe me, for certain people at least, not taking what one does not desire is the hardest thing in the world."

[8] *Alger-Républicain*, December 1, 1938. Title: "The Men Who Are Crossed-Out of Humanity." Subtitle: "57 Forced to Leave Algiers for Prison." See *Notebooks 1935–1942*, December 15, 1938.

This life (empty) of cities and unbearable days without love.

For ten years it is what has interested me more than anything else in the world.

The First Man. "And thinking of all that he had done without really wanting to, that others had wanted—or, more simply, because in similar circumstances others had done things this way—all of which nonetheless accumulated in the end to form a life, the one he shared with all men who ultimately die without having known how to live the life they really wanted to live."

The First Man. Theme of energy. "I will conquer, but without compromising. Compromise, hypocrisy, base desire of power, all of that is too easy. But I will truly dominate, without making a movement to possess or to have."

The only law of being is to be and to transcend oneself.

Jonas. The concierge beside herself (her son died): "Ah! Monsieur Jonas, you understand, don't you!" and then immediately afterward: "Don't go see Monsieur Jonas, he beats his wife and children."

The First Man. Theme of friendship.

M., without much culture and entering full-on into the masterworks. Incapable of dawdling with mediocrity, even out of laziness, and discerning greatness by instinct.

The First Man. Theme of anguish. (cf. Connaissance de l'homme.[9] Adler p. 156). Character motivation: desire for power, psychologically speaking.

Don Faust (or Doctor Tenorio): "I never asked anything for what I gave, I never spoke of what I did, I considered myself too small for never having given quite enough, and I thought mainly of all that I'd never given. But today I need the little that I've done; I need those who are here. Those to whom I've never refused my hand nor my help, they who speak and testify in my favor. *All are silent.* Then it is I who will speak. This one . . ." (rebellious text).

First Man. With Simone. For one year, he cannot take it. And then avoidance. She cries and this triggers everything.

Everything comes from my congenital inability to be bourgeois and a contented bourgeois. The smallest appearance of stability in my life terrifies me.

In the end, my greatest advantage over the disingenuous is that I am not afraid to die. I hold horror and distaste for death, but I am not afraid to die.

Treason of the left-wing intellectuals. If their true goal is to preserve the U.S.S.R.'s revolutionary principles while progressively correcting its perversions, what reason would the Russian government have to renounce its totalitarian methods if it knows in advance that they will always be excused? In truth, only the frank opposition of the West's leftists can make this government reconsider, assuming it can or wants to. But in truth our intellectuals' treason is still explained by something other than stupidity.

[9] Alfred Adler (1870–1937), *Understanding Human Nature.*

Why weakness in the face of pleasure would be guiltier than weakness in the face of pain. Weakness is sometimes responsible for incomparable devastation.

Don Faust. 1st scene or prologue – Faust asks to know all and have all. "Thus, I will give you seduction," the devil says. And Faust becomes Don Juan.

Last scene. He has to pay. "Let's go." No, the devil says, he must come against his will, otherwise he dies simply. "Die simply then" (here a chorus of men welcome the hero among them – Better late than never).

Russia and the communists' insular complex (Cf. Adler: Connaissance de l'homme, p. 154).

In N.R.F.: dialogues (answers, questions) or an imaginary letter[1] out of Actuelles.

Novel. "This evening did not go well—at the concert he applauded after the third movement thinking that the symphony was finished. But the vigorous and reproachful hush taught him that there were four movements. And the looks of his neighbors, heavy with recent ecstasy and sudden scorn, still pursued him."

One of the short stories in the French style (Jonas).

Flooding of the Seine. During the night, a noise from the river, never heard.

---

[1] Several times Camus employed the literary technique of writing imaginary letters. "Lettre à un jeune Anglais sur l'état d'esprit de la nation française" ("Letter to a Young Englishman on the State of Mind of the French Nation") was printed in *Alger-Républicain* in 1939. At the same time, in the *Notebooks*, Camus jotted a "Lettre à un désespéré" ("Letter to a Man in Despair"). And, of course, "Lettres à un ami allemand" ("Letters to a German Friend"), intended for the clandestine press and published in English in the collection *Resistance, Rebellion, and Death.*

Don Juan. The atheistic moralist finds faith. Consequently everything is allowed since someone can absolve what men cannot pardon. Hence, generous libertinism crowned with vibrant faith.

The taste of creation is so strong that those who are incapable of it choose Communism, which assures them of an entirely collective creation.

Theatre. Timon – Possessed – Julie – Impromptu – Press – Bacchantes.

Dante allows neutral angels in the quarrel between Satan and God. He slips them into the vestibule of his hell.[2] III 37.[3]

February 17.

Arrival in Algiers. From above, in a plane that runs parallel to the coast, the city looks like a handful of glittering stones thrown along the sea. The Hotel St. Georges' garden. O welcoming night toward which I finally return and which faithfully receives me as in days gone by.

February 18.

Beauty of Algiers in the morning. Jasmine in St. Georges' garden. Inhaling the scent fills me with joy, with youth. Descent on the city, cool, airy. The glittering sea from afar. Happiness.

---

[2] This line also appears in *The Fall*.

[3] ". . . that contemptible chorus of angels who were neither rebellious nor faithful to God, but thought only of themselves. Heaven drove them out so as not to lose its beauty and the depths of Hell rejected them, because the damned would draw some glory from them."

François' death, crippled. Sent back home from the clinic with tongue cancer. Dying alone in his hovel, vomiting blood all over the wall, he slams his fist against the thick and soiled wall separating him from the neighbors.

19.

In my home, not even one sofa. A handful of chairs. Always like this. Never neglect nor comfort.

Visit with Belcourt's merchants. 3 dead. The Massons. Marthe. Alexandrine. Juliette. Zinzin (prominent ears, contortionist, sings with the Alcazar cinema).

First Man.

In what year was Papa born?

I don't know. I was four years older than he.

And you in what year?

I don't know. Look at my family record book.

Well, his family abandoned him. At what age? – I don't know. Oh! he was young. His sister left him. How old was his sister? I don't know. – And his brothers? He was the youngest—no, the second. – But then his brothers were too young to take care of him. – Yes, that must be why. – Then, they couldn't have done otherwise.

At age sixteen, a farm laborer's apprentice for his sister's in-laws. They work him hard.

"He no longer wanted to see them. He'd had enough."

Id. He fights for the Arab cause. He is caught with his wife in an anti-French riot. He kills her to prevent her from being raped, but he survives. He is judged and condemned.

Or else: I fought 20 years for them, and the day of their liberation they killed my mother.

Id. X.'s suicide. St. Germain-des-Prés. Friends of Mephisto.[4] Marinella. Intoxication. Jean-Pierre insults X.: "You succeed in everything. You make me sick."

20.

Tipasa. Rain and sunshine. The wormwoods soaked in water. And streaming light, cool on the damp ruins. Same emotion, always new.

How lucky to be born into the world on the hills of Tipasa and not at St Étienne or Roubaix. To know my luck and receive it with gratitude.

21.

Radiant day. In the distance the sea and sky glitter, evenly mixed together. As every morning, the garden and the scent of jasmine, today the birds exult.

February 22.

Fog.

February 23.

Awakened by the sun flooding my bed. A day like a crystal cup overflowing with an uninterrupted blue and gold light.

February 24.

Orléansville.[5] In the morning, the mountains carved out in a delicate cyclamen petal. In Orléansville itself, shanties

[4] Cellar club in St. Germain-des-Prés, which was run by a Frenchman originally from Algeria.

[5] On September 9, 1954, an earthquake ravaged Orléansville. The town planner, Jean de Maisonseul, an old friend of Camus', took him along to see the construction site. A theatre was later built there and named Théâtre Albert Camus.

and reconstruction: the Far West. The young team of architects escapes despondency because they can see this city in the future.

February 25.

R.U.A.[6] The happiness of this simple friendship that I have lived.

February 26.

When the old queen has given birth to the young queens, they kill her or drive her out. And on the edge of the hive she dies of hunger.

This ridiculous parade of love and its abominable demands, thanks to which the weak and vulgar help each other to live and to appear.

April 26.

Departure from Paris.[7] Heartbroken and emptied of any joy by X. The Alps. And the islands that come one by one to meet us on the sea: Corsica, Sardinia, in the distance Elba and Calabria. Cephalonia and Ithaca are almost invisible in the twilight. Then the Greek coast, but at night, Peloponnesus's muscular hand becomes a dark and mysterious continent, covered with snowdrop, where here and there the snow-covered peaks shine. A few stars in the still illuminated sky and then a crescent moon. Athens.

27.

Awakening, wind, clouds, and sun. Some errands. My charming 21-year-old translator, with a youthful glow (I told

---

[6] Racing University of Algiers, where, in his youth, Camus was a soccer goalie.

[7] Camus flew to Athens, Greece, finally fulfilling a trip originally planned in September 1939, but canceled due to the war.

you I was close to the hotel but that was not true, and I ran the whole way so as not to be late, which is why I am out of breath), who wins me over and whom I adopt.

Acropolis. The wind has cleared all the clouds, and the whitest, most natural light falls from the sky. All morning, the strange feeling of having been here for years, moreover, of being at home, without even being bothered by the language differences. While climbing the Acropolis, this impression increases when I notice that I go there "as a neighbor" without an emotion.

Up there it's another thing. Over the temples and the ground stone, which the wind seems to have also stripped to the bone, the eleven o' clock light falls fully, bounces, shatters into thousands of white and searing swords. The light digs into the eyes, causes them to well up, enters the body with a painful speed, empties it, opens it to a sort of full physical violation, cleanses it at the same time.

Helped by habit, the eyes open little by little and the extravagant (yes, it's what strikes me there, the extraordinary audacity of this classicism) beauty of the place is received in a purified being, cleaned with the light's cresol.

Then the dark red poppies I have never seen before, one of which grows directly on a bare stone, alone, the [. . .],[8] the mauves, and marked by the perfect vantage point, space all the way to the sea. And the face of the second Kore statue on the Erechtheion, the bent leg of the third . . .

Here one fights against the idea that perfection was reached then and that the world has not ceased to decline since. But this idea ends up crushing the heart. It is again, and always, necessary to fight against it. We want to live and to believe that is to die.

Afternoon, Hymettus, a violet color. Penteli.

7 p.m. Lecture. Dinner at a taverna in the old quarter.

[8] One illegible word.

28.

Morning. With Margarita Liberaki.[9] Daphni. But Byzantium, definitely. . . . The place is charming. In Eleusis one must have a lot of imagination. But the fields before and after Eleusis are quite beautiful. In the temple, two paths lead to the sanctuary and the second is deviated such that everything is out of the view of the uninitiated.

Vital importance of what I know of Eleusis. To develop.

Admirable pieces at the museum.

Lunch at the embassy. Tiempo perdido.[1]

Afternoon. Agora. Theseion. Areopagus; in Agora's small museum, statues of Herakleion, Athena, Hercules. Hercules is knotty and hard beneath the flowery honeysuckles that cover him. Then I go up on the Hill of the Muses. The sun, low on the horizon, is not yet the red color that will draw it perfectly in the clear sky. But it is no longer intense: it wanes and loses its form. Then from its broken circumference escapes a subtle honey that spreads throughout the sky, gilds the hills and the Acropolis, and covers the scattered city blocks with a soft and unique splendor which reaches out to the four corners of the horizon, all the way to the sea.

I return just in time for my controversial lecture. After two hours of answering questions, I leave fatigued. Dinner in Piraeus with Margarita Liberaki. Curious being: secretive and grim with sudden bursts of life and laughter.

29.

Morning. National Museum. It contains all the world's beauty. I knew the Kore statues were going to touch me, but

[9] Greek novelist and dramatist.
[1] Lost time.

the wonderment with which they've left me lasts still. I am allowed to visit the cellars where they kept some of them during the war to protect them from the invasion and destruction. And there, in the cellar where history has thrown them, they still smile under the dust and straw that covers them, and this smile, over twenty-five centuries, still warms, informs, and encourages. Funerary steles, too, and repressed grief. On a black and white lekythos, the inconsolable dead cannot resign themselves to never seeing the sun and sea again. I leave unhappy and a little drunk with this perfection.

Then I leave for Sounion. The midday light is still slightly shrouded, carrying an invisible mist in the air, but I admire the space and vastness of these landscapes, however reduced. As we approach Sounion the light becomes fresh and youthful. Then on the cape, at the foot of the temple, there is nothing but wind. The temple itself leaves me cold. This marble, too white, has the appearance of stucco. But the promontory—where it rises and moves into the sea like a poop deck from which one controls the squadron of offshore islands, while in back, on the right and left, the sea foams along the flanks of sand and rocks—this is an indescribable place. The furious wind whistles so strongly in the columns that one would believe oneself to be in a lively forest. It swirls the blue air, sucks up the fresh sea wind, violently blends with the fragrance rising from the hill covered in miniscule fresh flowers, and furiously, without truce, snaps woven blue cloths of air and light around us. Sat at the foot of the temple to shelter ourselves from the wind; the light immediately cleared in a sort of immobile gush. The islands drift in the distance. Not a single bird. The sea foams softly all the way to the horizon. Perfect moment.

Perfect, except for this island across from Makronisos,[2] empty today it's true, but it was once a deportation island of which I'm told terrible tales.

All the way at the bottom, on the small beach, we have a lunch of fish and cheese in front of the large fishing boats in the small port. Toward the middle of the afternoon, the colors darken, the islands solidify, the skies lighten. This is the perfect moment of light, of abandon, where *All is well*. But because of my lecture, I must leave. I tear myself from these places with sadness and I never leave them completely.

But on the promontory again, before taking to the road, one sees Makronisos. Throughout the entire trip back, the most beautiful light that I have had here, over the fields of olive trees, fig trees with particularly green leaves, rare cypresses and eucalypti.

Lecture. Dinner where I obtain information on the deportation. The figures seem to agree. The number of deportees was reduced to 8 or 900. It is with this that I should be occupied.

30.

National Museum. Again I go to see the large and lean Kouros statues. Repetition of Hecuba. Except one, these young Greek girls lack grace and style. Dinner in Kifissia; beneath the soft light the garden resonates with the nightingales' song.

Afternoon. Work, then the Hill of the Muses. This time the sun is close to setting. Again a sort of hilarious joy before the

---

[2] In the political dossiers of Albert Camus' archives there is an important document about Makronisos.

extraordinary audacity of the Acropolis, where the architects played not with harmonious measures but with the extraordinary extravagance of the capes, of the islands thrown on the immense gulf, and of a vast, swirling, conch-shell sky. It is not the Parthenon that they built but the space itself, and with a delirious view. Over this entire squadron of islands and peaks, dominated by the rock's poop deck, the appeasement of night falls suddenly and [. . .][3] on a noiseless navigation.

Inserted Letter.

My dear X.

My current silence interests only me. It touches too many parts of my personal life for me to explain it to you. Nonetheless, you will be delighted to know that if I had spoken I wouldn't have said what you hope for, I wouldn't have given that pleasure to anyone. Besides, the cause that interests you does not lack appointed lawyers (I recognize, moreover, that they have not been very vigorous in the circumstance). But your letter pushes me to say one thing that I've wanted to say to you for a long time now. Namely that in the grand conflict that cuts the XXth century in two, you have already chosen.

For example, you know that East Germany has been rearmed for a long time and that a certain number of old Nazi generals are active there, just like in the West. On several occasions the U.S.S.R. has recognized Germany's right to have national forces. You say nothing of this. It is because you accept this rearmament if it is controlled by the U.S.S.R., but you refuse it within a Western framework. And it is like this with everything. In extreme cases (ask yourself), you would accept the transformation of France into a popular democracy

---

[3] One illegible word.

under the Red Army's protection (and I remind you that I defended—me—the communists against all "atlantization" of domestic policy). Every time that you spoke or wrote to me of these problems, your implicit opinion was obvious, your indignation only sincere in the face of Rosenberg-type crimes,[4] but as soon as it was about the repression of a worker's rebellion in Germany, courtesy of a communist regime, this created a sort of silence in you, filled with doubts (this last point is important and it seems to me a painful but decisive test of left-wing intellectuals).

Thus, in my opinion, you have chosen. And since you have chosen, it is normal that you enter the Communist Party. It is not I who will reproach you for it. I don't have contempt for communist activists, although I believe them to be making a fatal error. I have an excess of contempt for the intellectuals who are not really intellectuals, who murder us with their pseudo-ripping of secular priests, and who, finally, give themselves a clear conscience at the expense of the working activists.

Then, once and for all, do what you wish to do—straighten yourself out with yourself. You'll see then. You constantly compare two things of which you only know and judge one—the society in which we live—and you ignore the other. The Communist Party will not help you know popular democracy. Far from it. But it will help you know Communism, of which you know very little. If you find peace there, a rule of life, this will be all for the better. If not, at least you will have found there a true understanding of the question.

Solely to avoid any error, I repeat to you what I believe. German rearmament must be condemned in both cases,

---

[4] In 1953, Julius and Ethel Rosenberg, convicted for espionage, were executed in the United States, while in East Berlin the rebelling workers watched Soviet tanks repressing their movement.

otherwise everything is a deception. And if I continue to find helping Franco or the "fruit-bearing" policy in South America or colonialism inexcusable, I do not accept the fruit-bearing policy grafted on France courtesy of Russia and its unconditional supporter: the French Communist Party. In general, I remain fundamentally opposed to the initiatives and methods of what I've called Caesarian socialism.

Besides, these are things that you know. My books have simply meant much less to you than you say. Your sympathy for me was more real. But the one who enters into religion, he also loved his friends and his mother, and yet he abandons them. For I cannot let you believe then that you are not entering a church the second you choose an orthodoxy like that of the Communist Party. Do not doubt, but on the contrary, recognize in your heart that communist temptation is, for an intellectual, of the same nature as religious temptation. There is nothing shameful in it, provided that one loyally submits with full knowledge of the facts. As for me, you maintain, even from afar, my friendship. I only ask that if you take action on your project, when you hear that I am, objectively, as one says, a dreadful fascist, don't deny it, which will be impossible, but try not to think it. Good luck, from the bottom of my heart, and believe in my faithful thoughts.

The popular evening dances at "Johnny le fou."[5] I make an effort to find these dances interesting but the dancers, particularly the female dancers, are too unattractive.

May 1.
Early morning departure for Argolid. The Corinthian Gulf coast. A shimmering light, ethereal and jubilant, inun-

---

[5] Crazy Johnny's.

dates the gulf and offshore islands. Stopped a moment at the edge of the cliff, the sea's entire immensity ahead of us, offered in a single bend, like a caesura where we drink the light and air, in long gulps.

After an hour on the road I am literally drunk with light, head full of flashes and silent cries; within the heart's den, an enormous joy, an interminable laughter, that of knowledge, after which anything can happen and everything is accepted. Descent on Mycenae and Argos. The Mycenaean fortress is covered with thick bunches of poppies, which tremble beneath the wind above the royal tombs. (Every part of Greece I have traveled through is at this moment covered with poppies and thousands of flowers.) Above the fortress, the plain stretches up to Argos and the sea. Agamemnon's kingdom is no bigger than ten kilometers and yet the proportions are such that never has a more immense kingdom extended under the sun. Mycenae—sunk between its two high boulders, surrounded by enormous blocks, beneath a light that becomes frightful here—is today the savage queen of this unforgettable land.

The ruins of Argos are without much interest for me. The young archaeologist, Georges Roux, Vauclusian, so alive, so impassioned by his beautiful trade, he interests me quite a bit. I envy him a little and bitterly reproach myself for the wasted time of these last years and for my profound failure. We lunch in Asini, and before the lunch I swim in a crystalline and cold water on the beautiful beach.

In the afternoon, in Epidaurus, the May 1st festival has brought a kermis of joyous Greeks. But from above the theatre, in a thick and tepid light that spills over the slopes of olive trees, eucalypti, [. . .][6] and acacias, every sound resonates in a sort of vast and gentle disaffection. Only the

[6] One illegible word.

weak bells of sheep herds make themselves heard above the other sounds, but always with the same disaffection. Here, the hour is still perfect.

Soiree. Nafplion before the sea, at this hour, which the Greeks call the royalty of the sun and which is the hour of crimson in the sky, of mauves and blues deposited on the mountains and bays.

May 2.

Depart for Sparta in the morning beneath a formidable sky. Each wide valley constitutes a kingdom of olive trees and majestic cypresses, arid mountains, every so often a village—Greece is deserted here—only the pink, green, and red painted herds of sheep travel it. Over the plain of Evrotas, Sparta, beneath the snowy Taygetus, stretches its fields of orange trees, their abundant perfume no longer leaving us. Over the ruins of Mystras, flights of turtledoves. A tranquil monastery with whitewashed walls, opened over the immense plain of Laconia to the well-rounded and well-separated olive trees, shivering beneath a tireless sun.

Upon returning, the descent on Nafplion, its gulf, the islands and the mountains, in the distance. Stop in Argos with the young archaeologists doing the excavations. Same impression as in front of the small group of architects who rebuild Orleansville and live there in a community. I have only been happy and at peace in a trade, a job accomplished with other men whom I can like. I do not have a trade, but only a vocation. And my work is solitary. I must accept it and try only to be worthy of it, which is not the case at this moment. But I cannot protect myself from a feeling of melancholy in the presence of these men who are happy with what they do.

We return to Mycenae; the sun has just gone down at the moment we reach the highest terrace. Between the steep peaks which dominate it, a transparent moon softly sails. But across from us, the darkened plain extends from the foot of the Blue Mountains of Argos all the way to the brighter sea on our right. The space is immense, the silence so absolute that the foot regrets having caused a stone to roll. A train chuffs in the distance, on the plain a donkey brays and the sound rises up to us, the herds' bells rush down the slopes like a whisper of water. On this wild and tender setting [. . .][7] is magnificent. Over the now blooming poppies, a light wind passes very close to the ground. The most beautiful evening in the world sets little by little over the Mycenaean lions. The mountains darken little by little until the ten chains, which are reflected all the way to the horizon, become a single blue vapor. It was worth the grief of coming from so far to receive this grand bit of eternity. After this, the rest is no longer important.

May 3.

Work in the morning. Depart for Delphi at one P.M. Always the same light but this time over less considerable heights, stony, without a tree. It's at this point that one realizes Greece is primarily a space made of curved or straight lines, but always sharply contoured. The entire earth outlines the sky and gives it its form, but the sky in turn would be nothing without these reliefs whose harmonious closure organizes its own space. This is why every mile has divided this place into the grand kingdoms: the surface of the earth is double that of the sky. Arrive in a sort of basin, a single

[7] One illegible word.

149

cloud that we watched swell for some time now bursts and blusters in only seconds. Solid hailstones pound the car with a deafening sound. Five minutes later, out of the basin, we once again find the sky clear and carry on cheerfully.

Delphi. Initially, most striking about the grandeur of the site is, at the bottom of the immense valley, this murky green river which pushes its muscular hindquarters [. . .][8] toward the sea. The olive trees are packed so tightly one against the other that seeing them from this height, they make only one quivering path toward the horizon. As for the ruins, the storm, which has also fallen on Delphi, has wet them. They appear more alive in the middle of the more vivacious flowers and greener grasses. A black eagle sails very high for a few seconds and disappears. Then the day lightens and from the high cliffs a tranquility that announces the night begins to fall. Return to the stadium from which I leave happy.

Evening. In a bouzoukia,[9] four Greeks kindly invite me to dance. But their steps are too difficult. If I had the time for it, I would like to learn. From my room, the valley fills with shadows all the way to the small strand of lights that border the sea. Surrounded by filmy scarves, the moon places a fine, powdery light over the mountains and shaded hollows. The silence, vast as space, is good.

May 4.

Depart in the morning for Volos. Rough mountains, then the plain of Lamia. More mountains, softer, greener beneath

---

[8] Two illegible words.

[9] Somewhat similar to American nightclubs, a bouzoukia is a Greek venue where live music is performed.

the rising sun—and this is the immense plain of Thessaly. The Vlachs' primitive huts—and the immense expanse. The East is not far. Volos. 80% of the houses have been destroyed or knocked down. The entire city is under tents. The sun weighs on the cloths and the dusty city. Few or no bathrooms. I wonder how they avoid epidemics. French lycée under the tents. And the sea quite close, slick and cool, at the edge of the ruined city. The mayor receives me in the courtyard near the ruined house. Intelligent and elegant character. Due to an offhand remark, a hairdresser arrives and cuts my hair in the courtyard, in front of everyone, with the most charming familiarity. Still in the city. The Mass celebrated outside, the hospital tent, etc. Return to Larissa by car. Railcar. Larissa to Salonica. During the night we travel parallel to the sea glistening beneath the moon. Arrival 11:00 P.M.

May 5.

Work. Lunch with Turner and Colonel Bramble[1] (or someone who strongly resembles him). Byzantine churches. The small convent with the peacocks. St. David, St. Georges. St. Dimitriu. The twelve apostles (St. Sophie of no interest). I am not very touched by Byzantine art— one must acknowledge it, though—but interested in this evolution that goes from the Vth to the XIIth century and which makes it possible to reconstitute a link between the Hellenistic period and the Quattrocento. For example, the mosaics and frescos of the twelve apostles are far from the stiffness and hieraticism of that art's first centuries. There one finds the beginnings of Duccio. A little later (in the evening) I question a specialist who teaches me that

[1] Character in André Maurois's novel, *Les Silences du colonel Bramble* (*The Silence of Colonel Bramble*).

the Byzantine artists emigrated to Italy after the fall of Constantinople.

Little by little, the Eastern influence will be eliminated in this way.

Evening. Lecture. Am touched by a registered girl.[2] Reception for the University students. During the night I rest on my room's balcony, to gaze at the port, the caiques, the sea's flowery quay, and to breathe the beautiful scent of salt and the night.

May 6, 7, 8.

Lunch with T. in front of the sea, atop a cliff. The hour is pleasant. Afterward, T. plays me the latest compositions. I must leave. Plane. The Sporades drift off below us in the glittering sea. Dinner Merlier.[3] At midnight D. comes to get me and we leave for Piraeus where M. Algadès and his attractive cutter await us. Good-natured man, delighted and cordial. We leave Piraeus under an ashen moon that illuminates the sea with a hot, irreal light. I am happy to feel the water hitting the hull and to see again a light foam slipping by both sides of the ship's stem. But after a moment we see the fog literally being born from the sea, layer upon layer, thickening and, little by little, blocking the horizon. It is cold and damp. Algadès claims that he has never seen this in the archipelago. He has to reroute the cutter to avoid two small islands. I go down to lie down. Impossible to sleep until six A.M. Two hours later I awaken and go back up on the deck. The fog is still there. Algadès and his mariner kept watch all night out of fear of running aground. But little by little the sun rises, shows itself, pale, breaks through the

---

[2] Questionable reading.
[3] Octave Merlier, director of the Institut français.

fog and finally dispels it. Around eleven o'clock we move (without sails because there is no wind) on a motionless sea in a glittering and delicate light. The air is so limpid it seems that the least noise could be heard from the far end of the horizon. The sun warms the deck and its heat rises little by little. Then the first island appears. We pass between Seriphos and Sifnos, because of the detour we made. On the horizon, Syros and the other islands take shape, all appearing like a sketch in the sky. On the inverted hull of the islands, the small villages fixed upon the slopes look like shells, pallid concretions left by the receded sea.

The small yellow islands like bundles of wheat on the blue sea.

We sail in the middle of these distant islands on an illuminated sea, which gently wrinkles itself, runs parallel to Syros at length; soon Mykonos appears and as the day advances it begins to become clearer, its snakehead that bends toward Delos still invisible behind Rinia. The sun sets as we find ourselves nearly in the center of a circle of islands whose colors begin to change. Faded gold, cyclamen, a mauve-green, then the colors darken and on the still glistening sea the island masses become a dark blue. It is a strange and vast calming that then falls on the waters. Happiness at last, happiness close to tears, because I wish to hold against me, to squeeze, this inexpressible joy that, however, I know must disappear. But for so many days it lasts faintly, today it grips my heart so definitely that it seems to me I should be able to regain it faithfully every time I wish to do so.

Night has fallen when we descend on Mykonos. As many churches as houses. All white. We wander in the small streets where colored boutiques open. In the pitch-black streets we come across the scent of honeysuckle. The moon shines faintly above the white terraces. We climb back aboard and I lie down so happy that I don't even feel my fatigue.

In the morning a divine light falls on the bleached houses of Mykonos. We raise the anchor for Delos. The sea is beautiful, crystalline and pure above the sea bed of which we already catch sight. While approaching Delos, we glimpse enormous bunches of poppies on the first slopes of the island.

Delos. The island of lions and bulls, representations of which cover this island of animals, but one must add snakes to it [. . .][4] and large lizards with dark bodies, but light green at the tail and head, and the dolphins of the mosaics. The marble that the lions are made of is eroded and pitted by the effects of the erosion, so much so that they appear to be made of rock salt, a little ghostly, they give one the impression that the first rains will dissolve them. But this island of lions and bulls is also covered with the brown and friable bones that are the ruins, and beneath these bones, suddenly, admirable and fresh discoveries (mosaics of Dionysus at rest).

The island of ruins and flowers (poppies, convolvulus, wallflowers, asters) also. The island of the mutilated gods of the museum (little kore statues). At noon, climbed to the top of Cynthe, and the surrounding gulfs, the light, the reds and the whites; the entire circle of the Cyclades turns slowly around Delos, on the sparkling sea, in one movement, a sort of motionless dance. This world of islands so narrow and so vast appears to me to be the heart of the world. And at the center of this heart stands Delos and this peak where I am, from where I can look beneath the straight and pure light of the world, at the perfect circle that borders my kingdom.

[4] One illegible word.

Returned later by rowboat, a ravishing Greek teenager, dressed simply on the quay. When the rowboat leaves the quay I wave to her and she immediately responds with a beautiful smile. On the cutter I undress and plunge into the transparent green water. It is ice cold, and I climb back up after some strokes. We return to Mykonos. Feeling of infinite freedom to travel the sea like this, in all directions, from one island to the next. And a freedom not at all limited by the fact that this world of islands has boundaries. On the contrary, this freedom exults in its circle. For me, freedom would not be to puncture this circle and sail toward Sumatra, but to go farther from this bare island to an island of trees, and from the rock to an island of flowers.

In Mykonos to shop. I preferred the city at night. We return to sea late. Strange sadness so similar to the sadness of love while watching Delos and Cynthe disappear little by little behind Rinia. For the first time I watch a land that I love disappearing with the painful feeling that perhaps I will never see it again before dying. Heartache. The colors again change over the sea and islands [. . .][5] the sails, which flap softly with a light wind. Hardly have we tasted the peace that rises from the sea toward the sky, that empties its light little by little, and already behind a rocky isle the moon rises. It rises rapidly in the sky, then illuminates the waters. Until midnight, I gaze at it, I listen to the sails, I inwardly accompany the movement of the water on the sides of the ship. Free life of the sea and the happiness of these days. All is forgotten here and all is remade. These marvelous days spent flying on the water, between islands covered with corollas and columns, in a tireless light; I retain the taste of it in my mouth, in my heart, a second revelation, a second birth. . . .

[5] Two illegible words.

In the morning, head wind, the sails whip, the heel increases and we head for Piraeus with the loud noise of water and fabric. Rain of light, drops of which fall and bounce back on the morning sea. Despaired to leave this archipelago, but this despair itself is good.

May 9.

Depart for Olympia. The road to the Gulf of Corinth. Beaches and gulfs. Swim in Xylokastro. This time it is the intensity of the trees, the waters, the fresh fruits of the earth. A little before Olympia, the hills are covered with fragile cypresses. Gentleness and tenderness of these places beneath a light that is, for the first time, a little grey. The tall pines and the remains of the temples to Zeus and Hera. The birds' cries, the day ending, the peace that soon rises from the dormant glen. At night I think of Delos.

May 10.

For the first time, the morning is grey on the Alpheus valley, which I see from my window. But a soft light falls on the stones, cypresses, and green prairies. Since Delos, I could feel nothing more than the peace of these hills, this soft shade, this silence nourished by the birds' soft cries. Museum. Along with the frescoes of Sifnos in Delphi, the height of classical sculpture. Next to Apollo or the three male figures of the East Pediment, or the different Athenas from the metopes, Praxitele's Hermes is a sugary success that stinks of decadence. Behind it, moreover, two superb, large-framed terra cottas representing a warrior and Zeus removing Ganymede are evidence of a superbly different art. Strange archaic bronze kore statues, griffins, figurines that seem to come straight from the East. Stroll. It rains lightly, and the tender and washed colors of the valley are gentle on the eye. Fascinated by the diversity of landscapes. In fact, everything that Greece attempts with landscapes, it succeeds at and leads to perfection.

In the company of the villagers and their gentle familiarity. Free in appearance and movement even though political freedom does not exist here.

Brief evening rain. I climb up on the hill through batches of aromatic flowers. Small village of Thronia. Miserable houses. Children in tattered rags although apparently in good health.

May 12.

Cool and bright morning. The shade beneath the trees surrounding the ruins is quite precious. The light is divine. Swim and lunch in Xylokastro. The clear water is not as cold but the air has become mostly transparent and all the mountains on the other side of the Gulf of Corinth are revealed with a strange purity. M. has a sumptuous smile in this landscape. And like this, the whole route, soon the gulf of Athens, the islands, from which we can make out each house and each tree. I cease noting here these pleasures which from now on overwhelm me. Chaste pleasures, sober, strong, like joy itself, and the air that we breathe.

Thission.

In the luminous and clear sky the moon's tip like a hawthorn petal.

Evening at R.D. The honeysuckles, the bay far off in the night, the mysterious taste of life.

May 13.

These twenty days of racing through Greece, I contemplate them now from Athens, before my departure, and they seem to me like a lone and lengthy source of light that I will be able to keep at the center of my life. For me, Greece is no more than a long glittering day extended over voyages, and also like an enormous island covered with red flowers and mutilated gods endlessly afloat on a sea of light, beneath a crystalline sky. To retain this light, to return, to no longer give in to the darkness of days . . .

May 14.

Depart for Aegina. Calm sea. Hot and blue sky. Small port. Caiques. Aphaia's ascension. The three temples that suspend a blue triangle in space: Parthenon, Sounion, Aphaia. I sleep on the temple's flagstones, beneath the columns' shade. Prolonged dip in a small, tepid cove in Aya Marina. On the port in the evening they sell large lilies whose scent suffocates. Aegina is the island of lilies. Return. The sun goes down, disappears in the clouds, transforms itself into a golden fan and then into a big wheel with blinding rays. The islands, which I permanently leave tonight, again drift away. Stupid desire to cry.

The Variguerez evening and the shadow puppets.

May 15.

Sunday. Byzantine museum. With the D.'s in Kifissia, then on the beaches of Athens. Stroll by the sea beneath a nice wind full of light. For me these are the last hours, the farewell to this country, which for weeks has poured the same long joy over us.

May 16.
Depart for Paris, heart aching.

Novel. He looked at the sparkling artillery shell, blinding beneath the sun, which hid the motor. And again the mysterious joy threaded through him, a fountain flowed blindly inside him. It was the joy of Delos, circular, red and white, whirling circle. In an airplane that was falling uncontrollably toward the sea, above the appearing grain, life began again, identical to the approaching death.

The Guest.
The prisoner picks the path to prison, but Daru had misled him, he had pointed out the path to freedom.

Novel. A conceited character who does not complain under distress, does not give into anything.

A privileged person who, as an adult, discovers the working life. What he gives up little by little. And this is never enough. Even becoming a workman cannot change that he was not born as such. Finally he must die for it.

I tried to be a complete man and bring everything together in me. And then . . .

First Man. Francine family. Wolfromm family.

From the whole of genius, the Romans only had it in what we call our armies.

History is made of blood and courage. Nothing to do. When the slave takes up arms and gives his life, he exercises his rule as master and he oppresses. But when the oppressed, for the first time in the history of the world, rules by justice, without in his turn oppressing, everything will end and everything will at last begin.

My essay on Grenier.[6] Difficult. It's like pulling logs from a brilliant flame one by one. And then we find ourselves in front of the blackened firebrands.

In Ancient Greece, those who wanted to obtain magistracy were not to have conducted any business for at least ten years.

Julia.[7] She believes she can live with her two loves. But when Guibert proposes she live with him and his two loves also, she cannot allow him what she allowed herself. But she cannot judge him. Hence her social disease.

Still enough tenderness to help. . . . This sort of devotion, however, supposes that conviction is useful. I have the opposite impression, and that is what disarms me.

Fierce suffering and sunshine, every day. He is cured and adores, alone, the blood god.[8]

Moderation and insanity. Moderation in her relations with others; insanity against herself; struggling, bending. And in both cases, both things at the same time.

Jesus had 300 million contemporaries. He would have 2 billion.

Nothing burns in hell except the self (St Catherine of Genoa).[9]

The only French industry that does not experience underemployment is cruelty.

First Man. Peace for such a long time. And then one day he agrees to fight and risk his life. His joy.

[6] The preface for the new edition of Jean Grenier's *Les Îles* (*Islands*), which was published by Gallimard in 1959.

[7] Note for the planned play on Julie de Lespinasse. See Notebook VII, pages 54–55 and Notebook VIII, page 112.

[8] Note for "The Renegade" in *Exile and the Kingdom*.

[9] St. Catherine of Genoa (1447–1510), author of *Dialogues of the Soul and Body* and *Treatise on Purgatory*.

In Italian *talento* means desire.

First Man. "Many years later, when, giving in to various fatigues, it happened that we occasionally left each other at night with the slight disillusion of not having really loved each other that particular day, the small gesture of victory that she used to make in front of her door while I was waiting at the car's steering wheel, waiting for her to disappear, connected this apparently lost day to the solid thread of our dogged love, saving it from any bitterness."

Id. Jessica's incredible harshness during breakups. The loss of love is the loss of all rights, even though one had them all.

Play. A man *appoints himself king* today.

Étienne.[1] Howls while awakening and when he is alone.

Finally (if a life is worth a life) the condemned himself justifies the death sentence. (Cf. Melville finally gives in with Billy Bud.)

November 6, '56.

Facing the constant threat of destruction through war—thus the deprivation of a future—which morals can allow us to live only in the *present*? Honor and freedom.

I am of those that Pascal moves deeply and does not convert.

Pascal, the greatest of all, yesterday and today.

---

[1] Étienne Sintès, Camus' deaf-mute uncle.

First Man. The friend Saddok.

1) Young militant – My comrade—crisis of '36.

2) Friend – Returns to the Moslem tradition since the other betrayed him. Marries according to his father's volition. Fears missing his unknown wife.

3) Terrorist.

Later a European friend has his wife raped and killed. The first man and this friend rush to their weapons, arrest an accomplice, torture him, then throw themselves in pursuit of the culprit, surprise him, and kill him. His shame afterward. History is blood.

Id. Resistance sequence. He would rather be an R.A.F. hero. Be killed from afar. And not be subjected to the presence, the cruelty, of the enemy. No, he dreams of gigantic battles in the blazing sky of the metropolises and he goes by Metro to dusty or muddy places, from Paris to St. Étienne.

Id. Scene in the Montmartre Suburbs. As blows from the S.S.'s pistol butts approach in the porte-cochere and frightened neighbors recriminate against the resisters, he sees himself: contempt on his face. But why scorn? He gets rid of the plate. When the S.S. have searched him, he leaves with a little shame. He discovers on himself a paper just as compromising.

First Man. Pierre, militant, Jean, dilettante. Pierre is married. They both meet Jessica. Jean and Jessica since the old mistress. In one of the intervals, she is with Pierre, whom she leaves and hurts, and who will make his wife suffer. Thus he learns, far from meetings, what justice really is. Jean, on the contrary, learns to love Jessica, and in this way he opens himself up to people. Pierre dies close to Jean (war, Resistance) who has hated him out of jealousy. And he helps with all his heart. He is the man whom she has loved at least a little.

Id. Discovery of love. Fascination M.A.

Giorgione, the musicians' painter. His subjects and his fluid paintings, without contours, that elongate, that feminize everything, especially men. Sensual pleasure is never dry.

Venice in August and the swarms of tourists, who flock to St Mark's Square at the same time as the pigeons, peck at impressions and give themselves vacations and ugliness.

Parma. And over there, the same thing. Here are these small places that I loved 20 years ago and that still exist, far from me.

Novel. Do not forget Italy and *the discovery of art*—and of religion suddenly revealed in its relationship with art.

Each time this peaceful heart. And yet this time, continuously exhausted, incapable of coolness or emotion. And yet San Leo[2] and the heart open on a beneficial silence. Dear Italy where I will be cured of everything. On the way back, the old smell of dusty pathways. White oxen with long Romagna horns drag squeaking carts. The scent of sun and straw.

San Leo—and this desire of mine to retire there—Make a list of places where I think that I could live and die. Always small cities. Tipasa. Djemila. Cabris. Valdemosa. Cabrières d'Avignon etc., etc. Return to San Leo.

---

[2] Village of Montefeltro, in Marche, at an altitude of 1,932 feet.

Urbino. These small, well-enclosed cities, austere, quiet, closed up around their perfection. At the heart of the heavy fortifications, the indifferent characters of della Francesca's "Flagellation" wait eternally before the angels and the haughty Madonna. Sansepolcro.[3] Christ is resurrected. And here he is rising from the tomb, savage militant. Piero della Francesca's new frescos. One must return to the Sansepolcro valley at the end of a life. Vast, even, beneath the calm sky, it keeps the secret.

I rediscover the sea, again, tepid and gentle on the muscles.

The weight of St Croix. Madonna del Parto[4]

At the end of my life I would like to return to the path that runs down the Sansepolcro valley, descend slowly, stroll in the valley between the wispy olive trees and the long cypresses, and in a house with thick walls and cool rooms find a bare room with narrow windows from where I can watch night descend upon the valley. I would like to return to the Prato garden in Arezzo one evening and again walk the guard path atop the fortress, watch night settling on this incomparable earth. I would like . . . Everywhere and always this desire for solitude, which I don't even understand and which is like an announcement of a sort of death tinged with the taste of the contemplation that accompanies it.

Rediscovering Piazza della Signoria in Gubbio and gazing for a long time at the rain falling over the valley. Seeing Assisi without tourists or Vespas and listening to the harmony of the stars on S. Francesco's upper square. Seeing

[3] Sansepolcro, in Tuscany, is Piero della Francesca's hometown.

[4] Fresco by Piero della Francesca in the chapel of the Monterchi cemetery near Sansepolcro. A protector of the parturient, the Virgin in the chapel is represented as being pregnant.

Perugia without the houses which are built all around, and thus, one cool morning, able to gaze at the hills' wispy olive trees over the borders of Porta del Sole.

But especially, especially, repeat on foot, with a backpack, the route from Monte San Savino to Siena, to walk alongside this field of olive trees and grapes, whose scent I smell, by these hills of bluish tuff that extend all the way to the horizon, to then see Siena spring up in the setting sun with its minarets, like a perfect Constantinople, to arrive there during the night, alone and without money, to sleep near a fountain and be the first on the palm-shaped Campo, like a hand that offers the greatest of what man has made, after Greece.

Yes, I would like to revisit Arezzo's sloping square, the shell of the Campo in Siena, and again eat from the heart of watermelons on the hot streets of Verona.

When I am old I would like to be given the chance to return to this road in Siena, which is equaled by nothing else in the world, and to die there in a ditch, surrounded only by the kindness of these unknown Italians whom I love.

August 22, 1955. San Francesco di Siena. 11 o'clock in the morning.

At the Siena museum, one of the many last judgments (Giovanni di Paolo).[5] On the right, two blessed friends again find each other amidst a group and raise their arms to express their joy. On the left, in Hell, Sisyphus and Prometheus, their pain prolonged.

---

[5] Giovanni di Paolo (1399–1482), Sienese painter. His *Last Judgment* is at the Pinacoteca Nazionale in the Palazzo Buonsignori.

Novel. Portrait of the scorpion. He hates the lie and loves the mystery. Destructive element. Because the necessary lie consolidates. And the taste of mystery leads to inconstancy.

Novel. Grasshoppers – Earthquake. Attack on the isolated farmhouse – Attack on Philippeville – Attack on the school – Typhoon over Nemours.

Sensual, victorious, at the heart of a life full of joy and success, he gives up, enters into chastity, because he has surprised two fifteen-year-old children discovering love on one another's faces.

He wanted to be ordinary, going out, dancing, having the same conversations and tastes as everyone else. But he intimidated everyone else. By his demeanor, one imagined thoughts and preoccupations that he did not have or that he had without agreeing to place them on display.

First Man. Obligated to flee Algeria, the mother finishes her life in Provence, in the countryside bought for her by her son. But she suffers in exile. Her words: "It's nice. But there are no Arabs." It is there that she dies and that he understands.
Title: The Father and Mother?

October 24, 1955.
Death threats. My curious reaction.

166

They are united beyond time. But the years pass and she no longer dares show herself to him in the naked light of Parisian mornings.

Algiers. January 18.[6]

This anguish that I dragged through Paris, and which concerned Algeria, has left me. Here at least one is in the struggle, difficult for those of us who have put public opinion against us. But it is in the struggle, finally, that I've always found my peace. The intellectual, by function, and no matter what, he has some, and especially if he meddles in public affairs only by writing about them, lives like a coward. He compensates for this impotence with verbal exaggeration. Only risk justifies thought. And then anything is better than this France of resignation and brutality, this swamp where I suffocate. Yes, I arose happy, for the first time in months. I've recovered the star.

My entire life, through everything that France has endlessly made of me, I've tried to connect with what Spain left in my blood, and what, in my opinion, was the truth.

January 21.
Threats for this evening and tomorrow.[7]

---

[6] On January 22, 1956, during a meeting in Algiers, Camus and other European and Moslem liberals launched an "Appeal for a Civil Truce in Algeria." See *Actuelles III* and, in English, *Resistance, Rebellion, and Death.*

[7] In the days leading up to the meeting in Algeria, Camus continued to receive death threats. During the meeting itself, protesters gathered outside reportedly chanted, "Death to Camus."

January 22.

Adoration. The enigma of the world.

January 27.

First Man. X. declares that *only* the C.P. has always done what was necessary for their comrades. Difference of the generations. They have everything to learn, too.

Every artistic doctrine is an alibi whereby the artist tries to justify his own limits.

St Augustine[8] lived in the totalitarian world: the late Roman Empire. Marrou[9] said: "The art of living in times of catastrophe." Two oppositions to Christianity come from the peasants and the aristocracy. The pride of belonging to the Church of Africa. Faithful for 14 years to this woman who gives him Adeodatus. St Paul's text makes him a man of the church.

"No more feasts nor orgies, no more sleeping around nor debauchery; cover yourself with the Lord Jesus Christ and no longer seek to gratify the flesh in its concupiscence."

Always struggles to defend his work against the invasion of external occupations. His image of the divine *Sun* that illuminates our spirit.

"An abundance of words does not go without sin."

---

[8] In 1936, for his Diplôme d'Études Supérieures, Camus wrote a dissertation, "Métaphysique chrétienne et néo-platonisme" ("Christian Metaphysics and Neoplatonism"), which dealt with St. Augustine and Plotinus. A full English translation of the dissertation can be found in Joseph McBride's *Albert Camus: Philosopher and Littérateur*.

[9] Henri Irénée Marrou (1904–1977), historian, studied Late Antiquity, and St. Augustine in particular.

Chaste fear and servile fear. "You will always be able to enjoy everything but you will never see my Face. Choose." Nobody always wants to enjoy everything.

Those who accuse the time of being a time of misfortune: "What they want is not so much an era of peace and quiet but rather the security of their vices."

XVIIth century, Augustinian century.

Novel. Portrait of V.D. She has big strong hands and, at the end of a thin elegant body, the feet of a dancer. Everything is action, unrestrained ferocity in the dance where she reveals herself completely.

She celebrates the anniversary of the day she got her car, puts the dress that she just bought at the foot of her bed every evening so that she can have the joy of seeing it when she awakens.

She does not express herself except in indefinite terms. She has to go pick someone up someplace so that she can go to another place where she has to do something . . . etc. Double or triple hidden lives (cf. X. "I have a lunch"). "I have impure thoughts," she says. And, about someone who does not truly inspire impure thoughts: "It's in the bag."

The men with whom she has had relationships, they appear to her to be of another race. "Like Zulus," she says. "How not to feel compassion before an intelligent man. Everything that he knows and sees others put up with because they don't know or see it." "Women expect from men all the happiness of their life." "Women who don't please are stingy with the only man whom they have. Only women who please are capable of generosity." "I don't love really young people, they're idiots. A man always believes himself superior to the woman whom he . . . I accept this sentiment from an intelligent man, not from a young imbecile." Her small car. "I cannot do without it; I love it with tenderness for all the freedom that it gives me." There she keeps the old and filthy slippers that she wears to drive, abandoning her elegant Louis XV heels. For that matter, she abandons her shoes everywhere, cinemas, restaurants, etc. Lovely feet of the dancer that she is. "In my neighborhood there are only grandmas and pellagra sufferers so people notice me."

She arrives at the hotel with her baskets full of makeup and toiletries, her long thin blond hair [. . .].[1]

"Let's be frank, fame is an aphrodisiac."

If she became a billionaire, more exactly, if she married Onassis, she would macerate in a gold or platinum bathtub—which would better match her hair—filled with the perfume of her choosing.

"I love my car more than my mother." She loves her era.

Her avidity to laugh. Her determination to seize everything, succeed in everything, to taste all of today's pleasures: ski, sea, dance, high life, commercial success. And clear in this frenzied desire. Because of him. "I have defense." Her words: "She spilled an omelet onto her head" (speaking about a blond); "she would wreak havoc in a herd of Jesuits"; "during her shtick she can do a handstand or skin the cat, either way she is applauded." Since I have a bandage on my finger, having cut myself: "that makes you look like a clumsy carpenter."

What I love about V., what makes her attractive: she sticks to her class, however unbearable, which is to say that she has figured out what she can give without complication (develop). V. and marriage. She will be faithful if she marries. She will owe that much to the poor guy who . . . etc.

One always sees her fresh young lady's petticoat when she sits down. "I don't understand these married women

---

[1] Four illegible words.

who harass their husbands. They have money, a father for their children, security, their old days insured, and they ask for fidelity in addition. They overdo it." And further: "In marriage the man has everything to lose, the woman everything to gain," etc., etc.

Don Faust and Doctor Juan.[2] Leporello. Nothingness.

Id. He makes himself an actor, theatre on theatre.

Id. Faust and the youth of women (cf. Dupuis).

Id. In love, I was not faithful to her, and I would be in love if she were unfaithful.

Leporello: Nothingness.

"Is that your new servant?"

"Yes, he is a philosopher. I bought him in Paris."

Id. Nothingness. There is a regret in you that bothers me. There is nothing, I tell you. This statue, you can invite it, you won't see it coming.

D.F. Are you sure of that? Invite it.

Leporello goes.

D.F. No (he hesitates). Yes.

Leporello clowns around with the statue.

D.F. decides on chastity, searches for and finds a chaste girl. A long time ago I would have converted. But I've always held back out of fear of what my friends would say.

The old doctor of the prologue is an atomic scientist. He could blow the world up. But he is not like that; he wants to learn and enjoy.

End. The Franciscans have locked him up in a monastery.[3] He denies their god and confesses to them. Adoration of the world being.

---

[2] See Notebook VII, pages 95–96, and Notebook VIII, pages 111, 134, 135.

[3] In April 1940, Camus noted that he learned from Larousse's encyclopedic dictionary that Don Juan was murdered by Franciscan monks.

The true creator, if tomorrow he were to find himself alone, he would know a depth of solitude that no era has ever imagined. He would be alone to conceive and serve a civilization that cannot be born without everyone's support. He would be suspicious that this civilization is on its last leg and that he is one of the last to know.

F.M. He has an answer to everything except decency.

Before the third stage: short stories for "A Hero of Our Times." Themes of judgment and exile.[4]

The third stage is love: the First Man, Don Faust. The myth of Nemesis.

The method is sincerity.

History, easy to think, difficult to see for all those who are subjected to it in the flesh.

The oppressed has no real duty because he has no rights. Rights only return to him with rebellion. But as soon as he acquires rights, duty falls on him without delay. Thus rebellion, source of rights, is by the same token mother of duties. These are the origins of the aristocracy. And its history. He who neglects his duty loses his rights and becomes the oppressor even if he speaks in the name of the oppressed. But what is this duty?

Novel. A deportee is forced to strip. While he undresses, a cufflink rolls into a corner; he goes to pick it up.

---

[4] Here is an outline of an overall work plan, something Camus often made. After the absurd cycle (*The Stranger*, *The Myth of Sisyphus*, *Caligula*, *The Misunderstanding*) and that of rebellion (*The Plague*, *The Rebel*, *The Just*), a separate work on the themes of judgment and exile—*The Fall*. The next cycle was to be on love and Nemesis who, for him, was the symbol of moderation.

Paris. Spring, late and sudden. All the horse chestnut trees covered with their wax candles.

M.: "How could I be jealous of a person whom I know will die and slip away from me forever. My true jealousy would be to want to die with him no matter what."

The Growing Stone. The cook – But he's not bad. One's enemy should be killed: has he not been?
D'Arras: He has been.
The cook: Here, we kill our enemies, and afterward there's the Good Jesus.

At Solidor's; a man, Barbara, does his drag routine (as a society woman) in front of the guests: his mother, his grandmother, and a young man who is the son of his current lover. The family is delighted.

July. Palermo.[5]
Three days of mistral had brushed, polished the sky to its most delicate base, a thin layer, transparent and blue, swollen with a heavy weight of gilded water . . . and as such, we waited for it to burst and for a wave of Vin Jaune to drown the earth beneath an exultant flood.

[5] During the summers of 1948 and 1949, Camus and his wife stayed in a house near Palermo, on the Isle-sur-la-Sorgue. They returned there on different occasions. Albert Camus' family, still living in Algiers, lived in this house for a while as Camus tried vainly to acclimatize his mother, Uncle Étienne Sintès, and brother Lucien (and his family) to mainland France.

July 12. Palermo.

About the mistral. The days are hot and I wait for the mistral to pick up. Then I went on the hill that was covered in aromatic herbs and minuscule snail fossils. The mistral descended from the north, sweeping the nearby mountains, brushing the sky to its base, mashing and cleaning the trees, howling in the countryside, keeping animals and people in the houses, prevailing at last. . . . Etc. And lying on the hill, crushing shells, in the violent bath of wind and sun . . . the celebration.

A.B. writes to me about Van Eyck's true history. Shortly after the theft, a priest attached to the chapter was suspected. He confessed. He had stolen the panel because he could not stand to see judges near the Adoration of the Mystic Lamb. Considering his intentions, he receives absolution by promising to reveal the panel's hiding place the day of his death. The day comes. Extreme Unction. He wants to speak, but his voice fades away. He utters unintelligible words and dies.[6]

Through the years, what I have always found at the heart of my sensibility is the refusal to disappear from this world, from its joys, its pleasures, its sufferings, and this refusal has made an artist of me.

Jean asks for fishing equipment, which I buy for him. Searches in vain for worms. Then finds some. Goes fishing. Catches six minnows and bursts into tears before their agony. He does not want to fish anymore.

[6] The history of the panel stolen from Van Eyck's altarpiece is utilized in *The Fall*.

July 22.

The light and full moon above the poplars. Luberon nearly white and naked in the distance. A light wind on the reeds. Maman and I gaze at this marvelous night with the same aching heart.

But she is going to leave and I always fear not seeing her again.

Nemesis. Thoughts centered on the history of those who despise time the most, its effects, its edifices, and its civilizations. History for them is what destroys.

End of July.

Nights full of moon and wind. The large [. . .]⁷ of Vaucluse.

It seems that in this country no party can sustain the patriotic effort for long. So the right gives up in 1940 and then the left sixteen years later.

Stormy night. This morning the air is light, the contours clear. On the hill flooded with cool light, a pink carpet of bindweeds. The scent of young cypresses. Do not deny anything anymore!

If you know nothing more than this: I would like to be better.

---

⁷ One illegible word.

Music on the South Atlantic transatlantic liner. Only music is equal to the sea. And certain passages of Shakespeare, of Melville, of [. . .].[8]

Anecdote (imaginary, I suppose) about Russia: Stalin commanded Krupskaya to cease all criticisms or else he would appoint Lenin another widow.

Novel's end. Maman. What was her silence saying. What was this mute and smiling mouth screaming. We will be resurrected.

Her patience at the airfield, in this world of machines and offices that is beyond her, waiting without a word, as old women have for millennia all over the world, waiting for the world to pass. And then very small, a bit broken, on the immense ground, toward the howling monsters, holding her well-combed hair with one hand . . .

If nothing will redeem our days and our actions, then are we not obliged to elevate them in the greatest possible light?

Novel. Étienne. Great sensitivity. The odor of eggs on the plates. Whence, micro-tragedies.

Paris. Beauty is perfect justice.

[8] One illegible word.

Freedom is not hope for the future. It is the present and the harmony of people and the world in the present.

The Revolution is good. But why? One must have an idea of the civilization that one wishes to create. The abolition of property is not an end. It is a means.

At the first snowfall, Tolstoy's paternal grandfather used to send his dirty Russian linens to Holland on the sleighs that returned a bit before spring with clean linen.

Tolstoy: "Political literature, reflecting the transitory interests of society, has its importance, yet, however necessary to the people's development, there still exists another literature that echoes the eternal preoccupations shared by all mankind, and which contains creations precious to the heart of the people, a literature accessible to the man of any class, of any time, and without which no vigorous population full of strength has ever developed."

Tolstoy had a bastard child with Axinia (peasant).

Id. Turgenev reads Fathers and Sons to Tolstoy who falls asleep.

Id. cf. the countess: "He disgusts me with his people" (she has recopied War and Peace 7 times).

Id. Tolstoy: "The merciless beatings depress me."

Id. "Madness is selfishness."

Id. Shakespeare. "An abomination is a booby trap."

The Optina Hermitage that attracted all the Russian writers was founded in the XIVth century by a reformed crook.

See Alexandra Tolstoy: Tolstoy: A Life of My Father, p. 302 and above all for me p. 444.

Tolstoy speaking of the Russo-Japanese war: "In a war with non-Christian people, the Christian people must be defeated." Id. in his diary: "A criminal desire to die." And at the moment of death: "Alexandra, do not lose courage, all is well."

Novel (end). She sets out again for Algeria where the fighting is (because she wants to die there). They prevent the son from going into the waiting room. He remains waiting. At twenty meters apart, they gaze at each other, one at the other, through three layers of glass, with small signs from time to time.

The world collapses, the East is in flames, people are torn apart all around her, and M. on a deserted beach at the farthest end of Europe, in a howling wind, racing the shade of the clouds on the sand. She is life, triumphant.

August 1956

C.[9] I love this anxious, wounded little face, tragic at times, beautiful always; this little being with attachments so strong but with a face lit by a dark and gentle flame, that of purity, of soul. And when she turns her back on the scene, insulted by her partner, then this slight unhappiness fades away, and her frail shoulders.

For the first time in a long time, my heart is touched by a woman, without any desire, nor intention, nor game playing, loving her for her, not without sadness.

---

[9] This entry, and many of those that follow, seem likely to refer to Catherine Sellers, an actress whom Camus had recently met and begun an intimate relationship with.

Novel. After loving Jessica for fifteen years, he meets a young dancer who has, with slight differences, the same talents, the same fire as J. And something is born in Jean that resembles the love that he had for J. As if he were still capable of beginning again (and as M.H., in the same position, had loved Jessica without saying so). But he is old, she is young, he still loves Jessica and the love that he had for her. He is silent. Gives up. Life does not begin again. Hardly had he discovered, or believed to discover, that he loved her when, terrified, he decided never to lay his hands on her. He would like it if those whom we begin to love could know us as we were before meeting them so that they could perceive what they have made of us.

Inserted letter.

I am old or I will be. I've spent half of my life as a man defending one person at the price of sacrificing another and perhaps a part of myself. What I've spent twelve years protecting, I cannot throw away for a few months or a few years of life. The person for whom I broke another person, I cannot break her in turn, like a mischievous child who mutilates all his toys one after the other.

I've always thought that love, that any feeling, always ended up resembling what it was at the very second of its conception. And what I've felt before you is love without possession, the heart's gift. Possession is added to love and it has a dimension but not sensual. . . .

It's there that perhaps we could rediscover a sort of alliance, a marriage known only to us, an engagement, an agreement.

Time no longer existed for me; 10 hours a day in the theatre basement beneath the rehearsal lamps' poor, and at the same time intense, light; fascinated, I followed over this small face which was lit from inside by another light, a day of suffering, all the emotions that the pain of living can produce on the human face. I was there, before what is most profound, wounded, solemn, and unarmed in man. And when we went out, the unpredictable rains or the gentle September nights were welcomed as they were, an immutable order, the backdrop for that which is agitated and suffered in the hearts of men and women, and which, alone for long weeks, made me alive and full.

C., novel character. Young Jewish deportee, served at the S.S. camp (X.'s sister). *She returns.* She becomes an actress: 1) because her capacity for derision becomes spectacular; 2) because this removes her from the world; 3) because she lives all the lives that will be forever preferable to what she has seen and done. And on her face: Belsen and pity. That is what they applaud.

Her awkwardness. Burn, stain, lose, etc.

Alone in the car after a long night's work, Paris deserted, and the long rain resounding over the steel plates above them. On this face lit only by the gleam of a streetlight through the windshield, the shadows of water droplets streamed on the glass, ran without end. Around this shadow they huddled in their sheet-metal house, and around them the street, the silent city, a continent, the world in flames, and he could not tire of looking at this face streaming with shadowy tears.

"Our gentle, secret, solitary vacations." He shook the tree branches above the walls, and water droplets rained down over his friend's surprised face. One by one he drank these droplets that shone like feverish and tender eyes.

Sunday, September 2, 1956.
The slow foundering and her drowned face.[1] Birth.

Monday.
Faithful rain.

Tuesday.
Pure donation. Without asking anything for oneself.

Thursday, 6.
Insurmountable fatigue and finally the confession of love.
I would like to be able to breathe—to be able to love her by memory or fidelity. But my heart constantly aches. I love you continuously, intensely. Her hand-kissing hurt him. Her irritating manner of always leaving something behind her.

C.'s father—a Jewish doctor – Remains in Paris under the occupation. Deportee died in Birkenau. Typhus. Crematorium: "I always think that he had gold teeth." Separated from his wife, violent, passionate, seductive. C. loved him. Her life starts upon disembarkation at the age of sixteen.

Paris, where sunshine is a luxury, where dying costs an arm and a leg, where there are no trees without a bank account. Paris, which wants to give lessons to the world.

---

[1] In the short story "The Artist at Work," in *Exile and the Kingdom*, Camus writes that Jonas, being questioned about his infidelities by his wife, Louise, notices that she has ". . . the look of a drowned woman, that look that comes from surprise and an excess of pain."

The theatre bursts the cities' walls. And these fleabags who wish to make the theatres scruffy, in the cities' image.

At fourteen years of age, C. escapes from her house in El Biar during the night, her sheets tied into a rope.

C. the heart starving for unhappiness. Her fury *against* her body.

Tragic love and that alone. Tragic happiness. And when love ceases to be tragic it is something else and the individual again throws himself in search of tragedy.

Industrial civilization, by stamping out natural beauty, by covering long stretches of it with industrial waste, creates and fuels artificial needs. Consequently, poverty can no longer be lived and tolerated.

Faust is rejuvenated in Don Juan.[2] The wise and old spirit in a young body. Explosive combination.

Id. Scene where Don Juan assists with his burial. Don Faust or the Knight of the West.

Dawn. A fable. The Don Juan of knowledge: no philosopher, no poet has discovered him. He lacks the love of the

[2] See Notebook VII, pages 95–96, and Notebook VIII, pages 111, 134, 135, 171.

things that he discovers, but he has spirit and sensual pleasure and he enjoys the charms and intrigues of knowledge—which he pursues up to the highest and most remote stars—until finally there is no knowledge left for him to chase, except that which is absolutely *painful*, like the drunkard who ends up drinking absinthe and aqua fortis. This is why he ends up wanting hell. It is the last knowledge that *seduces* him. Perhaps it will also disappoint him, like everything he knows. Then he would have to come to a stop for all of eternity, nailed to disillusion, and he himself would become the stone guest, desiring an evening meal of knowledge, a meal that he will never have. For the whole world of creatures finds not a bite to give to this hungry mouth.

Intellectuals for progress. They are the dialectician's knitting wives. With every head that falls they rethread the stitches of reasoning torn out by the facts.

Joanna the Mad[3] remained forty-four years in a small, windowless room—lit day and night by a lamp—from which she left only to go to the neighboring convent and to gaze at her husband's grave. Perhaps this is real life.

The businessman who has had enough and makes a clown of himself. But without leaving his house or his business. Simply, he dresses as a clown.

X.X. After long kisses: "How violent it is!"

---

[3] Joanna of Castile (1479–1555), mother of Charles V, sister of Catherine of Aragon. It is widely believed that Joanna suffered some form of schizophrenia.

Custine[4]: "The contradiction that exists between a burning soul and the uniformity of existence makes my life unbearable."

Id.: "Today so many words are nothing but a negotiation between truth and vanity."

The two greatest minds the heavens gave to the Romans— Lucretius and Seneca—committed suicide.

After Nuptials, Summer. The Festival. (1 – Soccer; 2 – Tipasa; 3 – Rome – The Greek Isles – The Mistral – Bodies – Dance – Eternal morning).

He loses his daughter. I am an old man now. To be young, one must have a future.

Massacre of the innocent during Christ's life. Born guilty, one must die innocently.[5]

Reprinting of Fall, p. 73: "melancholic surrender," p. 126 masculine corporation.

Dr Schnitzler. Several concentration camps. Saved finally because he was *likable*. Everyone helped him.

---

[4] Astolphe de Custine (1790–1857), French writer, author of *Souvenirs et portraits* (*Souvenirs and Portraits*).

[5] See *The Fall*: "The children of Judea massacred while his parents took him to a safe place; why did they die if not because of him?"

X.X. professor: "Men must love one another," "they must
. . ." "they must. . . ." Around him, reality: an indescribable
mess.

At times I feel myself overtaken by an immense tenderness
for these people around me who live in the same century.

The Canadian prostitute in a café near the Folies-
Bergère: "My father has been around the world, me too, trust
me, I was in Germany, in Algeria, I've suffered too much, I've
nearly starved to death, I'm lousy now and my mother hasn't
seen me for two weeks, my father jumped on a mine, my
brother also, in short, I do this for you because you're a good
pal, well, I wait for him, it's already enough that I make my
family run through money, still going out with that idiot, ah,
it's not going well, I don't know anyone."

N.: power in moderation is the highest power.

M. says: "The race of Christ—and the other."

Play. A writer (or savant or artist or actor) overworked
due to social pressure is overtaken *in life*. Beside him, a
quite dignified professor seized by love displays evidence of
infantilism: he claims to know how to drink, to drive cars,
make love, practice judo, etc.

In the world there is, parallel to the force of death and
constraint, an enormous force of persuasion that is called
culture.

In the Old Testament God says nothing, it is the living people who serve him with their words. It is because of this that I have not stopped loving that which is sacred in this world.

N. realized. Multiplication of experiences but controlled, oriented toward the greatest being and the highest epoch, by extreme freedom but according to discipline—and the life risked without truce, like a permanent sanction—an accepted and *prodigal* solitude, bowing only before the human being, secretly. Say no more but do make meaning of a higher word and speak only according to . . . (For the one who is losing his memory the journal is like an instrument of that asceticism.)

Custine: "Arab architecture is the art of effeminate people (cut out papers that confectioners use to cover their boxes of sugared almonds). He (Custine) cites the word of Volitaire or Diderot: 'The Russians rotted before they were ripe.'"

At 10 years of age, with his friends, Nietzsche founds the *Théâtre des Arts* where two ancient dramas, of which he was the author, are performed.

June 1957.
Festival d'Angers finished.[6] Happy fatigue. Life, marvelous life, its injustice, its glory, its passion, its struggles, life begins again. Strength still to love everything and create everything.

---

[6] Camus played a vital part in the June 1957 Festival d'Angers. He adapted and directed Lope de Vega's *Le Chevalier d'Olmedo* (*The Knight from Olmedo*) and staged *Caligula* as well. Also showing at the festival was *On ne badine pas avec l'amour* (*Camille and Perdican*), staged by Jean Marchat.

July 15.

Depart from Paris. Sleep in Guéret. This is the universe of the family nuisance.

July 17.

Cordes.[7] Silence and beauty. The solitude of this large house, of this ghost town. Time flows, delicate, in me, and breathing returns to me. Around Cordes, over the perfect circle of hills, the sky rests, tender, airy, and at the same time both cloudy and bright. At night, Venus, big as a peach, sets upon the Western hill with tremendous speed. It stops for a moment on the crest, then abruptly disappears, sucked up like a token in a slot. Soon the stars multiply and the Milky Way becomes creamy.

July 18.

It rains. This morning, the wild Aveyron Valley. Work. I no longer endure any attachment, so mad with freedom that more and more I deepen a solitude that can be dangerous. I continuously think of F., my grief.

Evening. Discouraged by myself, by my barren nature.

July 20.

A letter from George Didier's[8] boss telling me of his death in an automobile accident in Switzerland.

---

[7] Claire Targuebayre, Edmond Charlot's former collaborator in Algiers, had opened a hotel in a manor in Cordes, in the department of Tarn. Camus had written a preface to her book, *Cordes* (Édouard Privat, 1954). He went to the manor to rest after the Festival d'Angers and to prepare new theatrical projects, most notably with Jean-Pierre Jorris.

[8] George Didier, a childhood friend of Camus' who had become a monk, died in an automobile accident at Chaux-de-Fonds, in Switzerland, on July 9, 1957. See Appendix, page 222.

July 21.

Rain that does not let up for days. Profound and dry sadness.

July 22.

Letter from Mi,[9] who speaks to me about her family and their "scathing feasts." Telephoning the one she loves, 700 km away, she cannot find her words. "I was miserable and merry there."

July 23.

The truth. The truth!

July 24.

Beautiful and deserted countryside where each house encountered has fallen apart. In barns gutted and infested by nettles, old harrow's wheels rust; old and enormous spiders haunt this deserted kingdom. Rush toward the cities, the factories, the collective pleasures. Here a civilization dies slowly, around us, and the old houses testify to it. I tell M. who tells me that she does not have the impression of death but of waiting. Waiting for what? – the Messiah.

It is still raining; I am hungry for light as for bread and can no longer stand myself.

---

[9] Mi, a young Danish painter, was the last of Camus' serious mistresses. They met at the Café de Flore in early 1957. Not too much is publicly known about her, and she refuses, to this day, to be identified by anything other than Mi.

July 24.

Depart Roussillon. The sea. Leucate. Return the evening of the 25th.

July 26.

Superb mornings. Drunken swallows.

Those who are not curious: what they know puts them off from what they ignore (C.).

Buddhism is atheism that became religion. Renaissance *originating from* nihilism. Unique example, I believe, and priceless to reflect on for us who are wrestling with nihilism.

One cannot ask suffering to justify its reasons. One would expose oneself to empathizing with nearly nothing.

Cordes. Every evening I went to watch Venus setting and the stars rising in the hot night, above its bed.

The old English lady commits suicide. In her diary, for months, she noted the same thing every day: "Today, nobody came."

At the end of The Adolescent (and in the three variations) Dostoyevsky ironically puts Tolstoy on trial.

Cordes. August 4.
  Thoughts of death.

August 6.
  Visiting Cayla: a silent and solitary place around which the world comes to die. I understand better what I later read in Eugénie de Guérin's journal: "I would gladly make a vow of confinement to Cayla. No other place in the world pleases me like my home." And yet: "Where will I be? Where will we be when these trees grow tall again? Others will stroll beneath their shade and will see, as we see, the passing winds that will knock them down."

  The Old Believers in Russia thought that we carry a small devil on the left shoulder and an angel on the right shoulder. There is an idea for the theatre (for Don Faust?): the angel and the devil grow according to whether they are nourished. In general, one *or* the other is heightened. My character returns with two smaller characters *of equal height*. Their dialogues: between them, the character to the two creatures, the two to the character, etc., etc.

  "The lightest silk thread is more unbearable to me than a lead ball is to others" (N.). Alas, to me also.

  Svidrigailov from Crime and Punishment: "A small room filled with smoke, with spiders in the corners, and that is all eternity is."[1]

---

[1] In *The Notebooks for Crime and Punishment*, Dostoyevsky noted that Svidrigailov "believes in the future life, WITH THE SPIDERS, etc." (It is Dostoyevsky who emphasized "with the spiders.")

August 8, 1957. Cordes.

For the first time, after reading Crime and Punishment, absolute doubt about my vocation. I seriously consider the possibility of giving up. I have always believed that creation was a dialogue. But with whom? Our literary society whose principle is second-rate spite, where offense takes the place of critical method? Society in general? A populace that does not read us, a bourgeoisie mass, who, in a year, reads the press and two popular books? In reality, the creator today can only be a solitary prophet, inhabited, eaten by a disproportionate creation. Am I this creator? I believed it. More precisely, I believed that I could be it. Today I doubt it, and the temptation is strong to reject this incessant effort which renders me unhappy in happiness itself, this empty asceticism, this call that alerts me toward what, I do not know. I would do theatre, I would randomly write dramatic works, without worry, I would be free, perhaps. What do I have to do with estimable or honest art? And am I capable of what I dream? If I am not capable of it, what good is it to dream? To free me from this, too, and to consent to nothing! Others who were greater than I have done it.

August 12.

C.S. "It is not pain that must arouse the greatest pity but indignity. The most extreme misfortune is to feel ashamed. All of you seem to have lived through only beautiful sufferings, distinguished sufferings." It is true.

Emerson: "The secret of genius is to suffer no fiction to exist for us."

August 13.

Depart from Cordes.

Atonal music is always dramatic even though it wants to be in reaction against musical romanticism. Insignificance is always pathetic and dramatic. Id. for painting.

A comment about The Fall since they do not understand. Shaped by and ridiculing the modern attitude and this strange and salacious secular remorse of sin. Cf. Chesterton[2] "The XIXth century (id. the XXth) is full of Christian ideas gone mad."

Why Lenin never concerned himself with the masses. Cf. Sperber[3]: The left and Truman's Fourth Point.[4]

Id. Freud did not feel a medical calling, a "penchant for humanity's suffering."

Nemesis. Profound complicity of Marxism and Christianity (to develop). This is why I am against both.

The blind lovers, groping about, kill the blind husband.

Un Théâtre Ininterrompu.[5]

Religion's attraction for theatre people. The dream life and the real life.

I loved those places (luminous restaurants, dance halls, etc.) that men invented to shelter themselves from life. This wounded thing inside me.

---

[2] Gilbert Keith Chesterton (1874–1936), English Catholic writer and pamphleteer.

[3] Manès Sperber (1905–1984), writer, disciple of Adler and friend of Malraux. On October 29, 1946, he participated with Camus, Koestler, Sartre, and Malraux in a meeting to try to define a minimum for political morals. (See *Notebooks 1942–1951*.)

[4] The Truman Doctrine, enunciated on March 12, 1947, aimed at containing Soviet expansion and led to the Marshall Plan, a vast program to aid nations threatened by communism.

[5] Literally, An Uninterrupted Theatre.

Necessity and exaltation of opposites. The measuring place of contradiction. Sun and darkness.

At the age of fifteen, Nietzsche, his comrades in front of him denying Mucius Scaevola's[6] action, takes a burning coal from the stove without saying a word and shows it to his friends. He carries the scar from this his entire life.

Story about the brothel[7] (H. p. 48). Cosima should be condemned for having destroyed all the letters from N. to W. "Tragic knowledge and Greek gaiety." The Basel Cathedral's terrace where Nietzsche and Burckhardt[8] conversed. "A modern anchoritism—an impossibility to live in agreement with the State." Id. "Aristocracy of the mind must conquer the entirety of its freedom with respect to the State, which today holds science in bridles" – Id. The dreamer, lying on a tiger.

About the Louvre fire during the Commune, which makes him cry and destroys him for days: "Never, so sharp was my pain, would I have thrown a stone at these sacrileges, which are, to my eyes, only the carriers of everybody's sin. Sin on which there is much to think about." "Arrange for me to be buried like a loyal pagan, without lies." Sad without light, exalted since his return.

Plan for "ten years of meditation and silence." Idea of the "mask."[9] Praise for Napoléon in La Gaya Scienza.[1] Affair with

---

[6] These notes were taken by Camus during a reading of Daniel Halévy's *Nietzsche*. Gaius Mucius Cordus Scaevola is a legendary Roman hero (sixth century B.C.). He was captured while trying to kill the Etruscan king Porsinna, and rather than naming his accomplices he let his right hand burn, which is where he got the nickname *Scaevola*, the left-handed.

[7] In Cologne, seeking a hotel, Nietzsche was directed toward a brothel. In the living room, in front of the undressed girls, he sat down at the piano and, to general shock, burst forth with one of his improvisations.

[8] Jacob Burckhardt (1818–1897), Swiss historian, colleague, and friend of Nietzsche's at the university and in the Pedagogium of Basel. He embodied, in Nietzsche's eyes, a type of grand professor.

[9] "Give me another mask, a second mask!" (*Beyond Good and Evil*).

[1] *The Gay Science*, a book that was found in Camus' mud-caked valise at the scene of the car accident that killed him.

Mme V.P. in 1887, last letter to Rohde, shattering.[2] Rohde does not reply. "Lisbeth,[3] why do you cry? Are we not happy?"

I had much prevention against rationalism. But my colleagues' passion [. . .][4]

September 8.
Death of Robert Chatté.[5] Alone, in Villejuif Hospital.

To refuse to shine when one can shine, to appeal, etc. A little artifice is necessary, but artifice ends up eating everything. Moping (as long as is necessary) is ultimately more fruitful than chitchatting and going out for nothing.

What would be necessary: not only someone whom you love without asking anything of, but also someone whom you love and who gives us nothing.

Novel. Mi: in love she breathed like a swimmer and smiled at the same time, then swam faster and faster, beaching herself on a hot and humid shore, mouth opened, still smiling, as if by dint of caves and deep waters, water had become her element and the earth the arid place where, as a dripping fish, she cheerfully choked.

The greatest man, the greatest spiritual force: the most, the most concentrated [. . .].[6]

---

2 "I now have forty-three years behind me, and I am as alone as when I was a child."
3 Elisabeth Forester-Nietzsche, Nietzsche's sister.
4 Two illegible sentences.
5 Bookseller, close friend of Pascal Pia's.
6 Two illegible words.

Nietzsche. Irreligious through religion. Pascal—in his way – After all, according to Thomas, faith is courage of the mind.

Id. For him, Christ: the immoralist Savior.

Custine. "One day the sleeping giant will rise and violence will put an end to the reign of speech. In vain then, frantic equality will call the old aristocracy back to the aide of liberty; the weapon taken again too late, grasped by hands too long inactive, will have become powerless."

Id. about the French: "they would paint themselves as ugly rather than letting themselves be forgotten."

Don Faust. When he is transformed into Don Juan, the scene begins with the hearty laugh of a man backstage, which signals Don Juan's entrance.

Nietzsche. "Still a few thousand years on last century's track! – And in all that man will do, the supreme intelligence will be apparent—but in precisely this way the intelligence will have lost all its dignity. It will be, without a doubt, necessary to be intelligent, but it will also be such an ordinary thing that a nobler mind will perceive this necessity as a vulgarity. Perhaps to be noble will then mean to be mad in the head."

The Bible is born among the stones.

October 1st.

G.T.[7] visits before departing for Algeria to confide in me what she has done. One month ago in Algiers. Contacted by

---

[7] Germaine Tillon, ethnologist who stayed in Aurès from December 1954 until March 1957. Camus wrote an introduction for the American edition of her book, which appeared in English under the title *Algeria*.

emissaries of the F.L.N.[8] who propose to her a meeting with those in charge, who have questions to ask her regarding her booklet (Algeria '57), she accepts. Then meeting procedures: she waits briefly at a house in the Casbah where she is received by two women. Then two armed men arrive. They argue. G.T. explains her thesis to them, the reduction of a population to beggary, the bulk of auxiliary wages, which come from France, the metropolis, etc. (her opinion: politically valid, economically uncultivated). At this moment, the one who appears to be the leader says: "You take us for murderers." Then G.T. says: "But you are murderers" (this is shortly after the attack on the Casino de la corniche). Then the other's painful reaction: tears in his eyes. Then: "These bombs, I would like to see them at the bottom of the sea." "That is up to you alone," G.T. says. They talk about torture. I am the plaintiff, she says (she belonged to the commission on [the] network of camps). They reach [one] compromise: suppression of civilian terrorism in exchange for suppression of executions. Pretty much in the terms that I had proposed (but the follow up, alas . . .). The other man regarding nailings: "It's France." "Go tell that to your grandmother," G.T. says, "I was there. It's the F.L.N. and you know it." The leader motions to the other man in order to keep him silent. She learns shortly after that this is Ali la Pointe. While leaving she takes him by the tie and shakes him. "And don't forget what I said." And he responds: "No, M'dame."

2nd meeting after execution and she learns then that the leader is Yassef Saadi. Two weeks after this, he is arrested.

Also shows me the writings of 30 Arab students between the ages of 11 and 12 to whom their Arab teacher gave the

---

[8] The Front de Libération nationale (National Liberation Front), or F.L.N., was formed in 1954 as the main opposition to French rule in Algeria, and became a major force in the Algerian War.

subject: "What would you do if you were invisible?" All would take up arms and kill the French, either the paratroopers or the government leaders. I despair for the future.

That the slave is subjugated because he preferred life over death is historically inaccurate. Budapest.

October 17.

Nobel. Strange feeling of overwhelming pressure and melancholy. At 20 years old, poor and naked, I knew true glory. My mother.[9]

October 19.

Frightened by what happens to me, what I have not asked for. And to make matters worse, attacks so low they pain my heart. Rebatet[1] dares speak of my longing to order the firing squads when he was one of those whom I, along with the other Resistance writers, asked to be pardoned when he was sentenced to death. He was pardoned, but he does not pardon me. Desire again to leave this country. But for where?

Creation itself, art itself, its detail, every day and rupture . . . To scorn is beyond my powers. No matter what, I must overcome this sort of fear, of incomprehensible panic where this unexpected news has thrown me. For this . . .

"They do not like me. Is this a reason not to bless them?" N.

---

[9] Camus was eating lunch at Chez Marius with Patricia Blake, a young American woman he'd met in New York and formed intimate relations with, when a representative from his publisher approached the table to inform Camus of the news: he'd won the Nobel Prize. Soon after, he contacted his mother to say how much he missed her.

[1] Lucien Rebatet (1903–1972), collaborationist journalist who wrote for *Je suis partout* (*I Am Everywhere*), author of the *Décombres* (*The Ruins*).

The saints are afraid of the miracles they produce. They cannot love the miracles nor love themselves in the miracles.

Three suffocation attacks this month, aggravated by claustrophobic panic. Unbalanced.

The tireless effort I have made to join the others in common values, to establish my own balance, is not entirely useless. What I said or found can be useful, must be useful to others. But not to me who is now delivered unto a kind of madness.

December 29.

3 P.M. Another panic attack. It was exactly four years ago, to the day, that X. became unbalanced (no, we are on the 29th, a day away, then).[2] For a few minutes, a feeling of total madness. Then exhaustion and trembling. Sedative. I write this an hour later.

Night of the 29th to the 30th: interminable anguish.

December 30.

Continued improvement.

January 1st.

Anxiety redoubled.

January–March.

The major attacks have passed. Only a dull and constant anxiety now.

---

[2] At the end of December 1953, Camus' wife, Francine, slipped into a serious depression for which she was admitted to a clinic for treatment.

March 5.

Discussion with de Gaulle. As I speak of the risks if Algeria is lost and of the fury of the French Algerians in Algeria itself: "French fury? I am 67 years old and I have never seen a Frenchman kill another Frenchman. Except me."

Compare France with the rest. "After all," he says, "no one has come up with anything better than France."

1905 revolutionaries' song: "Brothers, toward the sun, toward freedom."

Sperber. The Achilles Heel, p. 202: "The idea of substituting a radical break for suicide is not new. The will to definitively disavow his own acts, to forever untangle himself from them, is often found in the dreams that men devote themselves to: that only the body's logic still connects to life and that nothing connects to beings, neither what they received from them nor even what they gave to them. This dream is born of a solitude capable of destroying everything, even the affection that a man can have for himself."

In front of Hegel, Kierkegaard brandished a terrible threat: to send him a young man seeking advice.

Dostoyevsky, after his admirable Speech on Pushkin[3]: "For what I said in Moscow, look how I have thus been treated almost everywhere in our press: as if I had stolen from or swindled a few banks. Ukhantsev (a famous swindler) himself does not receive as much garbage as I do."

Id. after his early success: ". . . created for me a questionable fame, and I do not know how long this hell will last."

[3] The speech was given on June 8, 1880, at the solemn meeting of the Society of Friends of Russian Literature, and was later published in *A Writer's Diary*.

"The thought that occupies me most is what our communion of ideas consists of, what are the points on which we will all be able to meet, regardless of predispositions . . ."
"One should not waste one's life for any goal" (extend).

Those who really have something to say, they never speak of it.

Marseille.
Algiers to *Kairouan.*[4] Double spray. The foam and crackle of the first wave to break against the ship—and all at once a violent wind blows, twists, wrings the air; and a second spray, not as thick with water, laced with a fine vapor, thickens the mist.

The seagulls' wings are broken exactly in the middle /\/\ in the shape of a rooftop.

The soldiers on the bridge, beneath the wind, pressed against the ropes, their heads wrapped with scarves, their capotes shapeless. These moments where man abandons demonstration and presses at the level of need, this is history.

Motionless over the upper bridge, the gulls descend and continue their patient flight close to me. The obstinate gulls with their globular eyes, their sorcerer's beak, their tireless muscles. The seagulls have nowhere to rest other than the waves' changing hollow or the tall mast's oscillating cross.

Condorcet: "Robespierre is a priest and will never be anything but that."

[4] Camus returned to Algeria in March and April 1958. He was received by the University of Algiers and met with the Kabyle writer and teacher Mouloud Ferraoun, who would be assassinated by the O.A.S. (Organisation de l'armée secrete) in 1962.

Among the *primary* reflexes, those that belong to man and animal's immediate nature, Pavlov listed the "freedom reflex."

Power does not separate itself from injustice. Good power is the healthy and careful administration of injustice.

Never speak of one's work.

Actor.

Nietzsche. "In a superabundance of vivifying and restorative forces, even misfortunes have a solar splendor and generate their own consolation. . . ."

Id.: "Supposing that we are always waiting for misfortune, for an unpleasant surprise, we will always be in a state of tension and animosity, will be unbearable to others and we will see our health suffering from it; such natures lead to their own extinction."

Id.: "Fear of death, European disease."

Id.: "Happiness lies in the swiftness of feeling and thinking; all the rest of the world appears slow, gradual, and stupid. Whoever could feel a light ray's flight would be filled with happiness, for it is very swift."

Id.: "Portrait of man to come: eccentric, energetic, cordial, tireless, artist, enemy of books."

Id.: "Men of very high culture, with vigorous bodies, are above all sovereigns."

About the biophages[5]: Montherlant's Notebooks, p. 82: everything there is said with excellence and moderation.

For me: I would have succumbed to every last one of my remaining feelings. I have always opposed two feelings, one to the other.

Tipasa: The sky grey and soft. At the center of the ruins, the slightly choppy swells come to replace the birds' chirping. The Chenouas[6] enormous and light. I will die, and this place will continue to dole out plenitude and beauty. Nothing bitter about this idea, but on the contrary, a feeling of gratitude and veneration.

Algiers' heavy, vertical rain. Endless. In a cage.

Algerians. They live in the richness and warmth of friendship and family. The body as the center, and its virtues—and its profound sadness as soon as it declines—life without a view other than the immediate one, than the physical circle. Proud of their virility, of their capacity for eating and drinking, of their strength and their courage. Vulnerable.

The stabbed dove.

---

[5] Biophages—the word is Montherlant's: "Those who corrode, who devour our lives are initially the indifferent ones to whom business obliges us to give sprigs of our time . . ."

[6] A mountain range near Tipasa, on Algeria's coast, as well as the language of a population living in a village on the mountain.

Return. Kairouan. Storm. Irresistible impulse to throw myself into the water. The solitude and resignation of a man alone in the raging seawaters behind a ship pursuing its path.

Stages of healing.

Letting volition sleep. Enough of "you must."

Completely depoliticize the mind in order to humanize it.

Write the claustrophobic—and comedies.

Deal with death, which is to say, accept it.

Accept making a spectacle of yourself. I will not die of this anguish. If I died from it, the end. Otherwise, at worst, shortsighted behavior. It suffices to accept others' judgment. Humility and acceptance: purely medical remedies of anguish.

The world moves toward paganism but it still rejects pagan values. They must be restored, to paganize belief, Graecize Christ and restore balance.

Wouldn't it be that I have suffered from the excess of my responsibilities?

Since I am in the desert and lifelessness, I must push aridity all the way to the end so that the threshold is reached and, one way or another, crossed over. Madness or complete control.

Method: as soon as the appearance of anguished breathing accelerated or slowed down the warning. Thereto *associating* immediate deprivation of *every action* and every gesture.

Second association: general relaxation.

In the long run: transfer and accumulation of the energy that is characteristic of all want or desire by the temporary suspension of this want and this desire.

With regard to society, recognize that I expect nothing from it. Any participation then becomes a gift that does not await repayment. Praise or blame then become what they are: nothing. Finally, suppression of the conformist.

Eliminate the brooding morals from abstract justice.

Remain close to the reality of beings and things. Return as often as possible to personal happiness. Not refusing to recognize what is true even when the truth happens to thwart the desirable. Ex.: recognizing that power, it also, it especially, persuades. The truth is worth all the torments. It alone establishes the joy that must crown this effort.

Recover energy—as the central force.

Recognize the need for enemies. Love that they exist.

Systematically shatter automatisms from smallest to largest. Tobacco, food, sex, emotional reactions of defense (or of attack. They are the same thing) and *creation itself*. Asceticism not out of the desire that must be kept intact, but out of its satisfaction.

Recover the greatest strength, not to dominate but to give.

May 3.

Almost a total recovery; I even hope for increased strength. Understand better now what I have always known: the one who drags through his life, and succumbs under its weight, cannot help anyone with the few duties he does take on. The one who controls himself and controls his life can be truly generous, and give without effort, expecting nothing and asking for nothing but this strength to give and to work.

Journal.

End of April 1958. Cannes.[7]

At sea every day. In the evening, the nets' buoys (a bottle with a lead clapper, the whole thing floating on cork) make the sound of bells gathering the sea's flocks. At night in the port the boat's masts and bridges shriek and whimper.

The light—the light—and the anxiety retreat, not yet gone, but dulled, as if put to sleep by the heat and sun.

April 30.

Martin du Gard. Nice. He straggles along with his rheumatoid arthritis. 77 years old. "In the face of death nothing prevails, not even my work. There is nothing, nothing. . . ." "Yes, it is good not to feel alone" (and his eyes fill with tears). We set a rendezvous for July at *Tertre*.[8] "If I am alive." But always this same heart interested in everything.

May 29, 1958.

My job is to make my books and to fight when the freedom of my own and my people is threatened. That's all.

The artist is like the god of Delphi: "He does not show nor does he hide: he signifies."

Chekhov: "I am neither a liberal nor a conservative. . . . My holy of holies is the human body, health, intelligence,

---

[7] During this stay at Michel Gallimard's, Camus uses Michel's boat, *Aya*, a twenty-five-foot speed craft.

[8] The name of Martin du Gard's property in Bellême (Orne). In 1955, Camus prefaced the Pléiade edition of Martin du Gard's *Œuvres complètes* (*Complete Works of Martin du Gard*).

talent, inspiration, love, and absolute freedom. The freedom from all brute force and all lies, in whatever manner they are expressed:

That is what my agenda would be if I were a great artist" (letter to Pleshcheyev.[9] 1888).

Musil[1]: a great project that supposes all the means of art, which he does not have. Hence this work is moving by its failures, not by what it says. This author's interminable monologue, where the genius shines in some passages, and where art never shines in its entirety.

Musil. "Each one of us possesses a second nature where everything that he does is innocent."

"Ordinary life is the average of all our possible crimes."

Maman. If we loved enough those whom we love, we would prevent them from dying.

June 9, 1958.
New departure for Greece.[2]

June 10.
Acropolis. The feeling is not as great as the first time. I was not alone, and so I preoccupied myself with my com-

---

[9] Alexey Pleshcheyev (1825–1893), poet, had been condemned to death alongside Dostoyevsky and was then pardoned at the same time.

[1] Robert Musil (1880–1942), Austrian writer. A translation of his *The Man Without Qualities* was published in French in 1957.

[2] Camus, with his longtime lover Maria Casarès, met Michel Gallimard and his wife and Mario Prassinos (who designed the original hardcover editions of Camus' books) and his wife and daughter for a boat trip in Greece.

pany. And then the meeting with O., which bothers me. The Acropolis is not a place where one could lie. At two o'clock, the airplane to Rhodes. Islands, rocks on the sea, drifting off behind us. Pulverization of continents. In Rhodes, we land in the middle of fields where short flowery wheat grows, which the wind moves in waves toward the blue sea. Sumptuous, florid island. The promenade at night, in the center of the Frankish architecture. Encounter with R. P. Brückberger, who announces to me his intention to break with the Church without defrocking. My liking for him always alive. Boat with Michel G. and Prassinos.

June 11.

I get off the boat in the early morning, alone, and go to wash on the beach of Rhodes twenty minutes away, alone. The water is clear, fresh. The sun, at the beginning of its trip, warms without burning. Delectable moments that remind me of Madrague mornings, twenty years ago, when I used to leave the tent sleepily, a few meters from the sea, to plunge into the somnolent morning water.[3] Alas, I can no longer swim. Or rather, I can no longer breathe as I used to. Nevertheless, I regret leaving the beach where I have just been happy.

At ten o'clock we leave Rhodes to pass the northern point of the island and to arrive near Lindos.

12:30 Lindos.

Small, natural port, almost enclosed. Perfect bay. We lose an anchor in the absolutely clear waters. Initially, the

---

[3] In July 1941, Camus lived in a tent for a week on the beach dunes of Madrague, close to Oran. See the preface of the 1958 edition of *L'envers et l'endroit* (*The Wrong Side and the Right Side*).

bay is dominated by the village's white houses, then by the Acropolis, fortified by medieval ramparts in the middle of which rise Doric columns.

We reach the beach in a dinghy. Swim. At the end of the afternoon we climb toward the Acropolis. Over the top, wide, steep stairs lead to an immense midair space, which on one side dominates the port where we are anchored, and on the other, a balanced, dizzying void, another enclosed cove, the one where Saint Paul landed. Above this space the swallows turn, drunk with light, plunge vertically into the void and climb back up with piercing cries. The day ends over the columns, the two bays, the capes that multiply all the way to the horizon and the immense sea before us. Feeling of powerlessness to join, to express so much beauty. But at the same time, recognition before the world's perfect state. Back in the city, the young donkeys, the rowboat in the evening . . . During the night, the donkeys' loud braying.

June 12.

At six o'clock I climb onto the deck one last time to see the bay that I love. Everyone on board is asleep except the captain. In the mild morning, the scent of Lindos, scent of froth, of heat, of donkeys and grass, of smoke . . .

Rhodes at 8:30 A.M.

Stroll to see a gorge full of freshly hatched butterflies. They are nestled in the grass, the trees, the caves, and before our steps they disperse in silent and bustling clouds. Crushing heat. Return. Depart for Marmaris, a Turkish port, at three P.M. Arrive at five P.M. The bay we are anchored in the middle of is beautiful but somber. The little town, from afar, looks pathetic. And little by little we see all the inhabitants gathering on the pier. The Turkish police and customs officers arrive on board. Interminable discussions to settle the customary formalities. Then we disembark and are surrounded by a crowd of disheveled children. The poverty, the dereliction of the streets and houses makes the heart ache so much so that we return without waiting any longer. After dinner, another visit from the officials. More discussions (they do not speak any Western language), interminable. They kept the passports, etc. We will get them at six o'clock in the morning. The captain protests . . . etc. We will actually have to go to pick them up the next morning.

June 13.

Depart at seven o' clock. At eleven o' clock, the island of Symi. Admirable Greek cleanliness. The poorest houses are freshly painted with lime, decorated, etc. Unbelievable and revolting that the Turks could have dominated these people for such a long time. Swim. But growing claustrophobia. For everything else, superb form. At three P.M. we again set out for Kos.

Kos. Small port where life is easy at night. Music. The radio's loudspeakers shout the events of Cyprus with a tone I know all too well. We dine beneath a pink light.

June 14.

The island. Small temple on a beach with clear water. Swim and lunch in Psameros. In the small cove, five houses painted with lime, white and blue. The little girls get in the water in their shirts and swim toward us.

Every day, the monstrous sun . . . not heavy nor veiled by mist, but clear and pure, hurling all its heat, ferocious . . . To Kalymnos at six P.M. The sea is covered with short, cool waves. . . . Dozens of children with round heads escort us. Katina. June 15, the following day, she runs all the way to the pass and again, for a long time, waves her hand. Noon swim in Leros. Then toward Patmos where we enter a bay that is almost entirely protected. The evening hour.

June 16.

Climb upon mules and donkeys toward Patmos and the Monastery of St. Jean de P. From up there, the two isthmuses. The violent northern wind (the meltem) picked up. The Greek mistral has the same effects: it brushes the sky and brings forth a purified light, clear, taut, almost metallic. But it prevents us from returning to the sea; we have to wait here until it calms.

June 17.

Depart at six o'clock in the morning under the meltem to head toward Gaidaros. But the sea is furious. Shaken for three hours by big waves—everybody on board sick or sallow—the boat is diverted to the Fourni Islands. Shelter in a deserted cove where the wind blows less, but it blows. Day of waiting. Toward the evening the wind dies down a little, but it is too late to leave.

June 18.

The wind, which picked up again during the night, now blows violently. We waive departure. Then, since nothing changes and the bread is running out—the water soon—we decide to leave around six P.M., regardless. Everyone in the cockpit. Heavy squalls, but we arrive in eyeshot of the fires of Tigani (ancient Samos) around eight-thirty P.M.

Gentleness of the small port, quiet in the night, after the violent sea.

June 19.

In the morning I go for a swim alone. Depart by car to visit the island. One of the most beautiful because of the great abundance of olive trees and filiform cypresses that furnish the slopes of the hills and mountains toward the sea. After having taken a dip, we lunch in a small village on the southern coast. The table is outside. A crowd of beautiful children play around us, then come to look at us. One of the little girls, Matina, with golden eyes, touches my heart. When we leave, she comes close to the car and I take her small hand. Toward the evening, the Heraion, the crushed temple whose formidable debris—scattered in front of the sea among the reeds and oats, in the middle of an admirable landscape of mountains and sea—has itself been destroyed by the recent earthquakes. In a nearby café, where our drivers offer us a drink, they begin to dance together to the sound of a radio, for their pleasure and ours.

Polycrates, tyrant of Samos, "brilliant statesmen and depraved tyrant." Frightened by his own luck—insolent, perpetual—and by his unflinching successes and his fabulous wealth, he threw an expensive ring that he wore on his finger into the sea in order to beseech fate. But a fish served on his table returned to him this ring that it had swallowed. Completed the Heraion, held a sumptuous court where the arts held great importance. Perished crucified by the strategic Croites who lured him into a trap (522).

June 20.

Day at sea toward Chios. In the morning a manatee beneath the bow. It rolls, moves forward, waddles with a mocking air, then plunges toward the depths. A little later, a few miles from shore, the scent of rosebays comes to us on the wind. Afternoon of sun and swimming in a cove where the water is ethereal due to its clarity; we enter Chios on a beautiful and quiet evening.

June 21.

Chios. Turkish quarter. Crossing the island. The enormous cinder-block houses. Red soil. Enormous olive trees. The peasants beating wheat with their mules' hooves, beneath a blinding heat. The summer of massacres.[4] Finally, the leprosarium, in a narrow ravine planted with eucalyptus, dead-ending in an impasse of rocks. Series of long dilapidated brown and dark green buildings. Retired in the unfolding evening to their rooms with large iron beds covered with coarse brown blankets. 11 leprous women and 3 leprous men roam beneath the verandas. Some have lost fingers. Others with large turbid eyes, yellow, without pupils or eyeballs, like an enormous, rotten drop of water. Their natural gaiety beneath their thick, greyish clothes of infinite poverty. One of them complains that somebody wants to remove them from this miserable place to move them elsewhere. . . . Evening dances and laughter very late into the night.

June 22.

Toward Mytilene. Vast indentation of bays and beaches. The olive trees go down almost to the sea. P. is sick. Doctor

---

[4] Allusion to the massacres in Chios perpetrated by the Turks in April 1822, which inspired Victor Hugo's poem "L'Enfant" ("The Child"), in *Les Orientales* (*Oriental Poems*), and Delacroix's celebrated painting *Scènes des massacres de Scio* (*Massacre at Chios*).

(Paritis). Ascent to Ayassos. Dip. I swim a little. Depart along the side of the island. At the end of the afternoon hundreds of terns, flying over the surface of the still water, again rise by the boat. Arrival at Sigris.

(We arrive in the ports at sunset. And at times the sun masked the port from us, then disappeared behind the hill, and in the twilight the port appeared. . . .)

Sigris. Return to Sigris. Two enclosed bays. Naked hills. Smooth water, evening light. The world and life end here. And begin again.

The village, viewed from the boat at night, is illuminated by Saint-Jean's fires.[5]

Depart during the night. Michel and I take the midnight watch. Night on the sea, immense after the crescent moon sets in the west. The constellations descend toward the horizon. Unforeseen islands take shape in the shadows on the horizon. In the morning, Skyros, layered over its crests.

Depart at three P.M. for Skopelos. In the afternoon, the Northern Sporades. One, two, five, ten, fourteen islands appear on the sea. Skopelos at night and its roofs' edges are underlined with lime. Jasmine, pomegranates, hibiscus. Peaceful night. In the morning Skiathos, and we take the Euripus Strait.

June 26.

Khalkis. Preface Grenier[6]: "each conscience wants the death of the other." But no. Master and slave. Master and

---

[5] A reference to the French celebrations, Les feux de la Saint-Jean, in honor of the summer solstice; often bonfires are an integral part of the festivities.

[6] See the preface to Jean Grenier's *Les Îles* (*Islands*): "Among the half-truths that our intellectual society is enchanted by appears this exciting one—that each conscience wants the death of the other. At once we are all masters and slaves, dedicated to mutual destruction. . . ." "Grenier, like Melville, indeed completes his journey with a meditation on the absolute and the Divine." See page 160.

disciple. History was built on admiration as much as on hatred.

For this book I want the young reader who resembles the one that I used to be.

Like that quest from island to island that Melville illustrated in Mardi, this one ends in a meditation on the absolute and the Divine.

Khalkis. At night, vast and silent Bay of Marathon. The waters suddenly settle. Only a brief and heavy surf. And night falls over the immense corrie of mountains and over the suddenly mysterious bay. Beauty sleeps on the waters.

June 27.

In the early morning, while the cicadas begin to shriek in the surrounding hills, swim in the still and fresh water. Then the sea and at twelve o'clock, Kea, the island with green rocks, large pasty oysters beneath the slightly veiled sky. But during the night the southern wind picks up, and the next day, the 28th, we are stuck in Kea. 29th. Depart in the morning on bad waters. Sounion. Light. Hydra, Spetsai for the night. 30th. Poros, Egine and again Ayia Marina like four years ago. Marvelous island at the center of a whirling of light and space. Return there.

July 1st.

Athens. Heat. Dust. Idiotic hotel. Fatigued. 2nd. Delphi. Again the extraordinary rise in light levels. I lay my feet in my footsteps. Evening scent over the small stage. 3rd. Return to Corinth. Until Patras. Alone, quick dip, the water . . . Patras: large, dusty Oran, ugly and alive. 4th. Olympia. 5th.

Mycenae, Argos. The tall pines of Olympia crackle with cicadas. Greece bursting with sonorous braying in the valley hollows, on the slopes of the island.

Pavese.[7] As if the sole reason why we always think about ourselves is that we have to stay with ourselves longer than with anyone else. As if genius is fecundity. To be is to express, to express constantly. As if idleness makes the hours slow and the years fast, and activity makes the hours brief and the years slow. As if all libertines are sentimentalists because for them the relationships between men and women are an object of emotion, not of duty.

Id. "When a woman marries, she belongs to another, and when she belongs to another, there is no longer anything to say to him."

Id. The old Mentina woman, who for seventy years has ignored history. She has lived a "static and immobile life." That gives Pavese the shivers. And what if the old Mentina woman had been his mother?

Live in and for the truth. The truth of what we are foremost. Quit compromising with people. The truth of what is. Don't be tricky with reality. Accept then its originality and its impotency. Live according to this originality until this impotency. At the center, creation with the immense force of the person finally being respected.

Return. Lunch with A.M. He tells me that Massu and two or three of his collaborators have submitted to torture in

---

[7] Michel Arnaud's translation of Cesare Pavese's diary, *Métier de vivre* (literally *Buisness of Living*, but published in English as *The Burning Brand*), had just been published in France. The passages noted by Camus occur on pages 86, 193, and 303.

order to have the right to . . . (The difference: they chose it. There is no humiliation.) Strange impression.

Since returning from Greece ten days ago, bodily strength and joy. Sleep of the soul and heart. In the depths, the convent sleeps, the strong and bare house where silence contemplates.

The lie lulls or dreams, like illusion. The truth is the only power, cheerful, inexhaustible. If we were able to live only of, and for truth: young and immortal energy in us. The man of truth does not age. A little more effort, and he will not die.

APPENDIX

[Albert Camus had attached drafts of letters and notes to Notebook VIII, which we publish here in the appendix.]

Letter to Amrouche

November 19

My Dear Amrouche,[1]

It's time—and health—that has kept me from responding to you. It was necessary to respond at length, and I wasn't even able to keep up with my ordinary mail. Today I am no better able to do so. But I don't want to delay in thanking you for your second letter, which touched me. I owe you, however, the truth about what I think. Personal questions cannot separate us. What are they in the face of what is happening and about to happen? But I was painfully shocked by what you wrote, on several occasions, about French-Algerians in general (in Le Monde and in Commune). You have the right to choose the positions of the F.L.N. For my part, I think of them as murderous in the present, blind and dangerous in the future. But even while placing yourself on this side, you must make the necessary distinctions, which you

---

[1] Kabyle poet and essayist (1906–1962). In February 1946, he published in his journal, *L'Arche*, Camus' "Le Minotaure ou la halte d'Oran" ("The Minotaur or The Stop in Oran"), which would later appear in the collection *L'Été* (*Summer*).

have not done. I have given up on trying to make a voice of reason heard publicly. I hope, against all hope, to one day be able to do so. But, in private, I must tell you my reaction, and you should not ignore the shooting, nor justify that they shoot at the French-Algerians *in general*, and thus entangled, shoot at my family, who have always been poor and without hatred and who should not be mixed up in an unjust rebellion. No cause, even if it had remained innocent and just, will ever tear me from my mother, who is the greatest cause that I know in the world.[2]

In this sincere language, I know you will again find an echo of past fraternities. Can they inspire you to work toward appeasement and assembly, rather than toward fratricidal separation; that is the wish that forms, from the bottom of his heart, your brother of birth and sky.

Albert Camus

Letter to Anonymous

April 3

Monsieur,

My poor health has delayed this reply, and I apologize for that. More than a year ago, after having recognized what irremediably separates me from the left as well as from the right with regard to the Algerian question, I decided no longer to associate myself with any public campaign on this subject. Collective signatures—these ambiguous alliances between men, which all, by the way, break apart—lead to

---

[2] A similar sentiment would famously be expressed by Camus on December 12, 1957, at Stockholm University where, according to the December 14 edition of *Le Monde*, Camus stated: "I have always denounced terrorism. I must also denounce a terrorism which is exercised blindly, in the streets of Algiers for example, and which someday could strike my mother or my family. I believe in justice, but I shall defend my mother above justice."

confusions that largely overflow and consequently compromise the objective they mean to serve. Even when this objective is valid, as is the case, I have consequently decided no longer to act except personally, under the conditions and at the moment that I deem useful, no matter what pressures are exerted upon me.

Moreover, I intend to handle the questions that interest you in a book that will come out soon and that will speak for me alone. In any case, I entrust this personal response to your loyalty, and ask you to accept my sincere regards.

Albert Camus

Letter to Guérin[3]

June 9, 1954

My Dear Guérin,

Your article from the Parisian (I do not read this journal and I am not subscribed to Argus) was passed on to me. No, it is not "ingratitude," nor "rigor," that I reproach you for. I do not like the place, nor the discourteous manner, in which they are expressed. I do not like either that you speak of things that you do not know, by which I mean to say of my life. If you knew my life, you would have kept silent about this point. But as for content, you have the right to say that you do not like what I publish and to say it openly.

What I reproach you for is an unspeakable breach of the custom whereby a personal letter cannot be published without the sender's authorization. I did not write to you, at the time when I did, so that my trusting letters, written with freedom of heart, would ten years later be laid out in public.

---

[3] Daniel Guérin (1904–1988), sociologist and author who wrote, most notably, on anarchy.

You have the right to divulge your own secrets to that public and to speak with complete freedom about those who were your friends, but you do not have the right to force those friends to divulge their own secrets. By reading those sentences of affectionate camaraderie, written to a friend in pain, in the place where you have printed them, an intolerable embarrassment has come to me and a sort of disgust that you should have perceived in advance and which I do not forgive you for having inflicted upon me.

I cannot, in any case, let you go unaware of my feeling on this point.

yours
Albert Camus

Letter to Anonymous

July 20, 1956

Madame,

I am very sorry about what you have told me. And even more so since it undoubtedly concerns, I assure you, a misunderstanding.

I might have met the doctor whose name you mentioned, but this name means nothing to me. Thus, he is not one of my friends. And in any case I do not know this doctor well enough that he could ever take the liberty to reveal a secret concerning a third party. Besides, supposing that this secret were divulged to me, to imagine that I could have used it without care is not to know me very well.

I assure you on my honor that the details described in The Fall pertain only to me. Your friend is not the only one who likes the high plateaus. I love them and I have lived there. Once tubercular, I in fact suffer from a pulmonary sclerosis that has made me claustrophobic. Those who surround me can confirm my fear of pits, caves, and all enclosed places, which comes from this quite personal infirmity. People often joke with me about my impatience with speleologists, about my sadness in the deep alpine valleys, etc. As such, every detail that struck your friend can receive an irrefutable explanation. As for the principle anecdote, you understand that I do not come to divulge secrets here. Let me, however, quote for you a sentence from a letter I received from one of my friends the other day: "Each one of us, without exception, thus has a girl in his life whom he did not rescue."

This is clear evidence, and your friend must convince himself of this evidence. You say that he has always read me with regard and particular interest. Then he is aware that I am unable to lie about such a matter.

It is on my honor, I repeat, that I assure him that he has nothing, absolutely nothing, to do with my character. He has not been betrayed by anyone, and if he is what I imagine he is, he will give back to his friends this confidence of heart without which every life is an exhausting unhappiness.

A primary cause of the doubt from which your friend suffers today is the exhausting life that we all lead, and particularly so for those who add the stress of a personal work to the interminable weight of modern life. How could I not understand? Sometimes my days end with clenched teeth, and I often have the impression of walking and working by pure will that alone holds me up. But in these cases we must agree to be easy on ourselves and our own nature. We must return to a more animalistic life, at rest, in solitude.

I hope that your friend, enlightened by my testimony, will again find rest and peace. I will then comfort myself in having, without having wanted to, rid a virtuous heart of its turmoil. For the time being I feel only sad to have done harm with one of my books, as I have always thought that art was nothing if, finally, it did not do good, if it did not help.

Letter to M. R.P.

M. R.P.

I received your letter very late, and the news of my friend's brutal death[4] that you've delivered to me hits hard even though it's all over with. Nevertheless, I want to thank you, from the bottom of my heart, for having thought of me. Didier was a part of my childhood and my youth, and when I encountered him again later as a man of religion, I had no trouble liking once again what he had never ceased to be. Because he had remained the same child, become the same man, with the same faith, purer and deeper, and with the same fidelity. The discretion and constant sensitivity that he brought to our relationship, far too distanced by our different lives, could only enrich and render our childhood friendship that much more tender. This end, so sudden, so unexpected, is a great sorrow for me. For the last few hours, the world has been poorer in my eyes. I am aware that for him death was only a passage; he spoke knowingly of a certain hope. But for those who, like me, have loved him without being able to share this hope, the grief is all-encompassing. You are right: he remains a memory and an example. Know that, with gratitude, I transfer a part of our long friendship onto those who have loved him and had the joy of living near him, and do not doubt my faithful feelings from now on.

A.C.

[4] See page 187.

In the hospital X. discovered something that I have always known (because of a similar experience [. . .][5] youth—because of other things as well) the solidarity of bodies, unity at the center of the mortal and suffering flesh. This is what we are and nothing else. We are this plus human genius in all its forms, from the child to Einstein.

No, dear Dominique, it is not humiliating to be unhappy. Physical suffering is sometimes humiliating, but the suffering of being cannot be, it is life, just like this happiness that Bernard speaks of in his text with a conviction that so violently moved me.

I hesitate to tell you, but what you must do now is nothing more than live like everybody else. You deserve, by what you are, a happiness, a fullness that few people know. Yet today this fullness is not dead, it is a part of life and, to its credit, it reigns over you whether you want it to or not. But in the coming days you must live alone, with this hole, this painful memory. This lifelessness that we all carry inside of us—by us, I mean to say those who are not taken to the height of happiness, and who painfully remember another kind of happiness that goes beyond[6] the memory.

Sometimes, for violent[7] minds, the time that we tear off for work, that is torn away from time, is the best. An unfortunate passion.

---

[5] Three illegible words.
[6] Unclear word.
[7] Unclear word.

Gal[8] and I at the time of the demonstration:

You're going to screw up

Well! You don't want to come?

Albert I'm going to smack you.

He is like my brother, and in my family whoever touches my brother is dead.

Fame is a convent.

X. Initiation by his mother's gymnastics teacher. Upon his mother's request, the gymnastics teacher arranges a course of sexual initiation for him (at 15 years old), then persuades her that it is better that the thing be done by an expert. . . .

X. His rotund comrade repeats a sentence from the novel he is reading: "Live each hour as if it were to be the last and most beautiful," and he writes: "That's it exactly." But, X. says: he doesn't even leave his room to visit the city, and he divides his time between fine meals and his bed.

At heart, X. says, we are like these Christians. Pagans, well, everyone, but we profess our paganism on the tip of the tongue, even him. Her companion—with his athletic [. . .][9]—cannot make love before the match, because he must keep his strength, nor after, because he does not have any left; for the same reasons, he does not go out. In the morning, he wakes her with a knee to the small of the back so that she will go make breakfast. . . . She: "I don't have

---

[8] Pierre Galindo, a friend of Camus' from Oran, was previously cited in the *Notebooks* in 1939, 1941, and 1950.

[9] Illegible word.

sex, I don't go out, I'm the maid, and this has gone on for
three years."

From the prison's ink
on the slave's chains
to the gentle faces of the executed
I write your name
Liberty[1]

The strokes of your letters are bars
your face is a bolt
fraternal to the executioners
On the gate's command
I write your name
Liberty

Liberty, betrayed liberty
Where are your defenders?
In the cellar's darkness
Your gentle eyes crackle
I write your name
Kalande dies

Writing is easy
dying is terrible
I write, I write
I write your adulterous name
Over yours which despairs

Oh! What have you done with my young
Kalande? We die naked

---

[1] This poem is a retort—in a derisive tone, because liberty was betrayed—to Éluard's
famous poem "Liberté" ("Liberty"). The last line, "In capitals of pain," is intended to refer
directly to Éluard as *Capital of Pain* is the title of one of his surrealist collections.

When your brothers kill you
I write your sonorous name
In an ink that disgraces

To bar the future
To scratch out the memory
I write your name
Liberty
In capitals of pain.

                        Pierre Serment

NOTEBOOK IX

July 1 9 5 8 – December 1 9 5 9

July 21. Alone all day to reflect. Evening dinner with B.M.[1] In M.'s place inside me, all day, an emptiness that upsets me. I write to her.

22.24.

Nothing. Recorded *Fall* on my tape recorder. Mi's letter ("violent and pure nights"). Wandered yesterday evening in St Germain-des-Prés—awaiting what? Spoke with a drunk painter "What do you do for a living—I'm not in prison—that's negative—no it's positive" and he swallows five hard-boiled eggs sprinkled with cognac. Distressed by my inability

---

[1] Jean Bloch-Michel (1912–1987), a companion of Camus' at *Combat.*

to work. Fortunately Zhivago[2] and the fondness I feel for its author. Gave up trip to the Midi.

25.

Nothing. Recording Fall. Possessed distributed. N.R.F. Dinner with A.C. His romance with M., impotent with his wife, which M. reveals to her. "He is better," she says—"that is" – "Well, he is not yet a man, but he is no longer an old man either." This pool of shadows over their lives. All lives. After having accompanied her back, I stroll in St Germain-des-Prés. I wait, stupidly. Ah! if the strength to work returned to me, it would be the light, finally. The little punks, dressed up like James Dean, and the gesture of the hand, like a spoon, their ring fingers arranging their genitals, apparently wedged too tightly in their blue jeans. I think of the naked brown bodies, ages ago, in my lost country. They were pure.

26.

Recording Fall. Barely begun the preface for Islands.[3] Dinner with C., lazy and cynical, turned only toward pleasure. But he is self-employed. Also, a second-rate writer. But he bears no resemblance to anybody. I leave him early. He goes to play poker, which bores me, and I go home. Earlier: a rather inelegant girl, pursued by an Arab, rejects him. "I am racist," she says simply.

27.

Finished recording Fall. Don Giovanni. Grey sky all day. Evening film about soccer's World Cup. The young Black

[2] Boris Pasternak, *Le Docteur Jivago* (*Doctor Zhivago*), Gallimard, 1958.

[3] Jean Grenier, *Les Îles* (*Islands*), Gallimard, 1932. The new edition was prefaced by Albert Camus and released in 1959. See Notebook VIII, pages 160, 213–214.

Brazilians crying after the victory and trying to hide their faces from the camera. As before, this still touches and moves me.

28.

Dinner B.M. A.C. joins us. A storm weighs over the city— and does not break.

29.

Algeria obsesses me this morning. Too late, too late . . . My land lost, I would be worth nothing.

July 30.

Solitary day. Shapeless work. The evening, through Nabokov, Narayan—who could be Gandhi's successor—explains to us the movement of villager and agrarian socialism in the Indies (Vinoba).[4] I admire, distantly. Back home, passing in front of the Aiglon, I see A.M.'s name on the illuminated marquee. I enter. Eleven years ago, I had happiness with her. Married now to an Air France steward, with whom she goes fishing. And she sings every evening.

July 31.

In the afternoon, A.M. comes to see me for a half-hour. In the daylight, I see the traces left by eleven years. She was 22 years old, therefore she is 33. But we laugh a lot together.

---

[4] See Lanza del Vasto, *Vinôbâ ou le nouveau pèlerinage* (*Gandhi to Vinoba: The New Pilgrimage*).

August 1st.

Lunch at Barrault's place in Chambourcy. The sky is constantly black from a storm that never breaks. B. again proposes to me the Dantchenko-Stanislavski[5] association. In the afternoon Colin Wilson[6] – A baby; obviously Europe has conquered England. "We must now communicate faith in [. . .][7] I know it well. This faith is mine; it has never left me. But I have taken the path of the era—with its frustrations—so as not to cheat and affirm after having shared in suffering and denial, just as I had actually felt it. Now we must transfigure, and this is what distresses me in the face of this book that I must make and that binds me. Perhaps the painting of a certain distress has completely exhausted the men of my age and we will no longer be able to speak our true faith. We will only have prepared the terrain for the boys who follow us. I say to C.W. and "if I did not succeed, I'll have been an interesting witness, at best. If I did succeed, I'll have been a creator."

In the evening I dine with A.E. and Karin, then stroll to Montmartre with just Karin. The gardens in the night, washed beneath the moon but dark. Karin is 18 years old. Parents divorced. She left Sweden, I don't know why, and earned her living as a model for a second-rate designer who exploited her. Thirty-five thousand francs for seven hours of work a day. The courage of these girls of the half-century, it always fills me with the same admiration. Beauty a little boyish, but slow, as if absent. Return. Her naturalness. She immediately advances her tender mouth, then leaves, precise and reserved.

---

[5] Founders, in 1898, of the Moscow Art Theatre.

[6] Colin Wilson, self-taught British writer, who had just created a new type of hero, a rebel, *The Outsider*—in other words, the Stranger.

[7] Two illegible words.

August 2.

I force myself to write this diary, but my reluctance is exquisite. I know now why I never kept a personal diary: for me life is secretive. With respect to others (and that is what pained X. so much) but also, life must be lived through my own eyes, I must not reveal it in words. Unheard and unexposed, like this it is rich for me. If I force myself to keep a personal diary at this moment, it is out of panic in the face of my failing memory. But I am not sure I can continue. Besides, even so, I forget to note many things. And I say nothing of what I think. Hence my long reflection in regard to K.

Saturday 2.

The evening, M. at the train station until Sunday evening. Fatigued and distant. Toward the evening she resuscitates and I am happy about this.

Monday 4.

Lunch M. Afternoon Doctor X. According to him, because I must save X.'s health, this makes me live "in a glass ball." His prescription: freedom and selfishness. Superb prescription, I say. And by far the easiest to follow.[8] Evening K.

Tuesday 5.

Afternoon M. Long conversation. Few people have gone further than her in the acceptance of life. The 6th. Go out in the evening with Michel, Anne, and M. Dance. The 7th. Again the feeling of distance from M. The most passionate

---

[8] Camus' wife, Francine, remained in a serious and prolonged depression, which was treated with, among other methods, electroshock therapy. Camus often felt unsure of how to live with his wife's condition.

person whom I have known is in fact the most chaste. Dinner with the Russian nurse and her nine-year-old girl at Brice Parain's[9] place. B.P., like all religious minds, tries to justify all misfortunes by the necessary atonement. I tell him that, in any case, we meet all that is worst in dialectics. He knows this. He reflects.

Friday 8.

Solitary day like most of the preceding ones. I try to organize my work. It has rained for 2 days. Letter from X.: "well-oiled and informal conversations" (on the telephone). Warm, free, truthful.

Sunday 9.[1]

Sick. Sunday the 10th. Monday the 11th. *La Corde.* I lie down and fall asleep with a dreadful headache. Bad night. During the day Mi telephones from Marseille; she runs from one city to the next, pursued by anguish and panic. I advise her to return to Paris.

Tuesday 12.

In the morning C. comes to see me. Wednesday the 13th. Lunch Char. We laugh a lot. Afternoon Ivernel.[2] Evening dinner and golf with M.G., Anne, and R.G. Evening on the prairies. Thursday the 14th. Ivernel on the telephone. He spent all night reading my adaptation of Possessed without

---

[9] Brice Parain (1897–1971), philosopher and writer, principal partner of Éditions Gallimard.

[1] The day and date are recorded here as written, though clearly a simple mistake.

[2] Daniel Ivernel (1920–1999), French actor, played in Camus' adaptation of Dino Buzzati's *Un cas intéressant* (*An Interesting Case*), but the role of Shatov, in *Les Possédés* (*The Possessed*), was played by Marc Eyraud.

being able to put it down. He agrees to play the part of Shatov. Evening dinner with R. Physically, he has been the same for the past 20 years. But since his nervous breakdown the drive has disappeared. He lives by heart alone, obviously. We bump into K. Her naturalness suffocates me (the unreserved hand and then come along, no why, I have an appointment) she eats nonstop.

August 15, 16, 17.

This whole period since the 2nd is in fact empty. One cannot write without recovering vitality and energy—the heart's health—even if what one must say is tragic. Particularly so. Finished Zhivago with a sort of tenderness for the author. It's not true that this book again takes up the XIXth century's Russian artistic tradition. It's much more gauche and modern in composition, with its continual snapshots. But he does better: he resuscitates the Russian heart, crushed beneath forty years of watchwords and humanitarian cruelties. Zhivago is a book of love. And of such love that it is poured out upon all people at the same time. The doctor loves his wife, and Lara, and others still, and Russia. If he dies, he is to be separated from his wife, from Lara, from Russia, and from all the rest.

People without name are near to me
Trees, children, and sedentaries
I am overcome by all of these
And that alone is my victory.[3]

And Pasternak's courage was to rediscover this true source of creation and to work at it slowly in order to make it gush out in the middle of the desert.

---

[3] A snippet from Pasternak's *The Poems of Doctor Zhivago.*

What else? the evenings of the 16th and the 15th, recorded
The Poems of Char with M. Night of the 15th, stroll along the
Seine. Beneath the Pont Neuf young foreigners (Scandina-
vians) are joined together around two of their own, a trum-
peter and a banjo player, and lie on the street, couples em-
bracing, listening to the improvisation. Farther, on one of the
benches of the Pont des Arts, an Arab has stretched out, a
portable radio by his head, playing Arab music to him. The
Pont de la Cité, beneath Paris' warm and hazy August sky.

For Julia. Guibert is the noble progressive. Mora the face
of the old world.[4]

August 18.
Lunch M. Meet again. Evening dinner R. Depression not
improved.

19.
Letter from X. which saddens me once again.

Evenings of the 21st–23rd.
Mi. Fills these days with beauty, with gentleness. Far from
taking me away from work, this long joy turns me toward it.
Her 22-year-old sister dies from liver cancer. Her father or-
ders her to admire the sunsets: "because you are an artist."

August 23.
Death of Roger Martin du Gard. I had postponed my visit
to Bellême and suddenly . . . I again see this man, whom I

---

[4] Note for the planned play about Julie de Lespinasse. See Notebook VII, pages 54–55,
and Notebook VIII, pages 112, 160.

loved tenderly, speaking to me in Nice, in May, of his solitude, and of death. He dragged his large heavy body,
hunched over, from the table to the armchair. And his good
looks . . . One could love and respect him. Grief.

25.

Dinner Brisville[5] (and Thérèse). B.M. (and Vivette[6]). Go
out for a stroll. The chapel and over the outer boulevards.
Sordid Paris.

26–29.

Giacometti's example. Ah! and then M. and her life:
"Those who, like us, knew extreme experiences very young
(including fame and love), and who, arriving at maturity,
want nothing more than life, simply."

29.

C. returns.

September 2 at Isle-sur-Sorgue. Best rule for this notebook: to summarize from time to time (2 times per week?)
the important events of the past period. Saturday the 30th I
saw Jamois[7] and agreed with her that I could not immediately present The Possessed in Montparnasse. Despite her
dryness and air of bitterness, she has charm, with her
proper sandals, her small, well-kept feet, her long body, and

---

[5] Jean-Claude Brisville, novelist and playwright, wrote *Camus* for "La Bibliothèque
idéale," Gallimard, 1959.

[6] Jean Bloch-Michel and his wife, the novelist, Vivette Perret.

[7] Marguerite Jamois, director of the Théâtre Montparnasse.

this beautiful, sad look. Telephoned Barrault afterward to tell him of my agreement. Sleep early. I don't sleep all night, fall asleep at 3 A.M., wake up at 5 A.M., eat a lot, and, beneath the rain, take to the road. I don't leave the steering wheel for eleven hours—nibbling a biscuit from time to time—and the rain doesn't leave me either until I reach the Drôme where it lets up a bit over the heights of Nyons so that the scent of the lavender comes to me, awakens me, and enlivens my heart. The landscape that I recognize nourishes me again and I arrive happy. The Isle where, in the scanty room at the Hotel St. Martin, I feel at once sheltered and pacified.

Meet up with René Char at the Isle. Sadness to see him chased out of his house and his park (where hideous H.L.M. buildings[8] now rise) and stuck in this small hotel room at St. Martin. In Camphoux, at the Mathieu's, Mme. Mathieu, an aged Clytemnestra, wears glasses. As for M. Mathieu, the estate manager became an impotent old man who can no longer even control his explosions. I take care of the rented house, a bit sad but charming, however, with its view of the Luberon. Surely it will not please X. But I try to make it more comfortable. 3 long walks with R.C. on the roads of the Luberon peaks. The violent light, infinite space, moves me. I would like to live here again, find a house that suits me, finally settle down a bit. At the same time, I think a lot about Mi and about her life here. At dinner, Mme. Mathieu says: "Even the swallows have become foolish. Instead of taking silt for their nests they take the crop soil. And for the first time in decades, twelve of the thirteen nests in Camphoux have been crushed along with their eggs" and Char: "one would hope that at least the birds would salvage honor."

---

[8] H.L.M. (Habitation à Loyer Modéré), literally "housing at moderated rents," was rent-controlled, government-subsidized housing, often in the form of large apartment complexes.

The 4th I am still awaiting a telegram or telephone call from X. telling me of her arrival with the children. It is Mme. Mathieu who tells me that X. will only stay here for four days and that her family will be in Paris. Anger and disaffection, which mount against her and against me, we who never stop waiting for signs of tenderness there where there are none and cannot be any.

September 30.

A month after looking around the Vaucluse for a house, purchased the one in Lourmarin. Then off toward St. Jean to find Mi. For hundreds of kilometers, through the scent of the grape harvest, elation. Then the great, foamy sea. Pleasure like those long waves, flowing, grating on. Depart in the morning for Paris and the pink briars in the pine forests. Still twelve hours behind the steering wheel, then Paris.

Visit from the writer *turned* miserable intellectual (the slum of the St. Denis suburb).

Pasternak. ". . . this live and throbbing element of aristocratism that, following Pushkin, we call the highest Mozartian principle, the Mozartian element."

J. de Beer. "Adultery should be punished by death. True lovers could then be counted." Even this is not true. Often, spinelessness is stronger than fear.

October 17.

Depart Vaucluse. I should sum up these 18 days, and I will do so.

October 18.

I disembark from the night train in the dry and cold mistral at Isle-sur-Sorgue. Fine and grand elation all day in the glittering light. I feel all my strengths.

19.

Incessant light. In the empty house, without any furniture, up for long hours gazing at the dead leaves and red woodbine, blown by the fierce wind, entering into the rooms. The Mistral.

27.

Return to Paris. During the night reassuring voices announce the names of the stations. Nation.

Do not complain. Do not boast about what one is, nor about what one does. If one gives, consider that one has received.

November 5.

Letter from E.B.'s husband telling me that his wife wants to commit suicide and asking me to intervene. I who so easily and often so senselessly feels responsibility toward people, I do not feel any in this case. That said, I must intervene.

November 7, 45 years old. How I wanted a day of solitude and reflection. Beginning now, this detachment will be realized at fifty. That day, I will reign.

Democracy is not the rule of the majority but the protection of the minority.

November 22.

Dinner with Char and St. John Perse. Islands. Afternoon Waldo Frank[9] in a dreary room.

December.

Possessed rehearsals.[1]

Cuny, who is my age, seems too old to play Stavrogin.

M. We change jobs, that's all.

L. – Yes, but women will escape us and we will die.

Mi. Her marvelous appetite.

March 3.

I struggle like a fish caught in the net's meshes.

March 17.

Death of Paul Oettly[2] at 69 years old. The next day his old mother (93 years old) commits suicide.

---

[9] American writer who dealt with the economic and social realities of his country, and whose many works were published in France between 1920 and 1930. In his *American Journals,* Camus said of Frank: "One of the few superior men whom I have met here."

[1] *The Possessed* was presented for the first time on January 30, 1959, at the Théâtre Antoine.

[2] Paul Oettly was Camus' uncle by marriage. He married Francine Camus' aunt. An actor and director, he was often involved with Camus' theatrical creations. His mother ran a boardinghouse at Panelier, close to Chambon-sur-Lignon, where Camus lived from August 1942 to November 1943.

Catherine is ill. I suspend my departure for the Midi. Heartache.

March 20.

Maman operated on.[3] The telegram from L. reaches me Saturday morning. The following night, airplane at three o'clock in the morning. 7 o'clock in Algiers. Always the same impression over this land of Maison-Blanche[4]: my land. And yet the sky is grey, the air gentle and spongy. I settle at the clinic on the heights of Algiers.

In the spotless room with bare white walls: nothing. A handkerchief and a small comb. On the sheets: her knotty hands. Outside, an admirable landscape that extends to the gulf. But the light and space bother her. She wants the room to be kept shaded.

She speaks of Philippe, to whom Paule has just become engaged: "His father is good, his mother is good, his sister is good. They are ancient people. He, he has done his duty. He has seen Paule to the petroleum and (gesture of two index fingers coming together). All the better."

"Later, when I am at home, the doctor will give me something to recover." She says "thank you monsieur Doctor." She cannot do anything: neither read, she does not know how, nor sew or embroider, because of her fingers, nor listen, since she is deaf. Time drips, heavy, slow . . .

---

[3] Camus flew into Algeria for a brief stay as his mother underwent a hernia operation.
[4] An Algerian airport.

Her lips have disappeared. But her nose, so fine, so straight—her large forehead, full of nobility, her brilliant black eyes in the bony and shining arch.

She suffers silently. She *obeys*. Around her the family sits, dense, mute, and waiting. . . . Her brother Joseph, younger by a few years, also waits—but as he would wait for his turn—resigned and sad.

March 23.

Bad night. It rains in the morning over the gulf and the hills. The wisterias: they filled my youth with their scent, with their rich and mysterious ardor. . . . Again, endlessly. They have been more alive, more present in my life than many people . . . except the one who suffers next to me and whose silence has never ceased speaking to me throughout half my life.

She says Vichy[5] for all mineral water.

The flesh, the poor flesh, miserable, dirty, faded, humiliated. The sacred flesh.

Léopold [F . . .][6] on Nietzsche: "the consent to the life that the union of patience and revolt led to is the highest peak of life."

This strange habit of preceding her name with the distinction Widow, which had been with her all her life, and which still appears on hospital papers today.

[5] A popular brand of mineral water derived from the springs of Vichy, France.
[6] One illegible word.

She lived in ignorance of all things—except suffering and patience—and she continues to absorb physical suffering today, with the same gentleness. . . .

The people whom neither the newspaper, nor the radio, nor any technology has touched. As they were a hundred years ago, and hardly more distorted by the social context.

It looks like I've had blood in my stool. No? Ah! Good.

The smell of syringes. The hill covered in acanthus, reeds, cypress, pines, palm trees, orange trees, medlar trees, and wisteria.

March 29.
Return to Paris.

Sophocles danced and played ball well.

"Detras de la cruz esta el demonio."[7]

Destroy everything in my life that is not this poverty. To lose everything.

Pasternak on Scriabin[8]: "Each one of us has known a similar moment in our life. To each one of us the revelation is offered, this gift of a personality promised, and, in its way, to each one this promise is kept."

Id.: "The greatest works in the entire world, while speaking of the most diverse things, in fact tell us of their own birth."

---

[7] "Behind the cross is the devil."
[8] Pasternak devoted a chapter of his *An Essay in Autobiography* to Scriabin.

Id.: "... one can, day after day, run to rendezvous with a bit of built-up earth, as if it were a living being."

Nietzsche. "No suffering could, nor will be able to drive me to give false testimony against life, *such as I know it.*"
Id. "Six solitudes are already known to him
But even the sea was not solitary enough for him ..."
On the use of fame as the camouflage behind which "the self can again invisibly play with and laugh at himself."
"Win freedom and spiritual joy, so as to be able to create and not be opressed by outside ideals."
Historical meaning is only a masked theology.
N. Northern man, suddenly placed before the sky of Naples, one evening: "And you could have died without seeing that!"
August 20, 1880, letter to Gast where he laments Wagner's friendship "... what good is it for me to be right about many matters."
The man with a deep heart needs friends unless he has his God.
The men who have "a long-range willpower."
It is through L'Esprit souterrain[9] that Nietzsche discovered Dostoyevsky in '87; he compares this with the discovery of Le Rouge et le Noir.[1]
In '88 he discovers Strindberg's Les Mariés[2]

[9] *L'Esprit souterrain* (*Notes from the Underground*). "A few weeks ago, I was still unaware of the name Dostoyevsky—I, a poor illiterate who does not read any 'journals.' A fortuitous gesture in a bookstore brought my eyes to *L'Esprit souterrain*, which had just been translated into French (it was by similar chance that I found Schopenhauer in my twenty-first year, Stendhal in my thirty-fifth!). The call of blood (or how shall I call it?) became audible immediately; my joy was extraordinary." Nietzsche, letter to Overbeck, February 23, 1887.
[1] *Le Rouge et le Noir* (*The Red and the Black*) is a novel by Stendhal originally published in 1830 and later translated into English. Since then it has appeared in several different variations of this base title.
[2] *Les Mariés* (*Married*), a collection of short stories by August Strindberg, who was charged as blasphemous.

April 1st.

Love on the contrary, but impossible. *Search* no more? Receive it. Ultra-powerful in creation.

Nietzsche in '87 (43 years old): "My life is, at this very moment, at its meridian: one door closes, another one opens."

April 28.

Arrival Lourmarin. Grey sky. In the garden, marvelous roses weighed down by water, luscious like fruits. The rosemary is in bloom. Stroll, and in the evening, the irises' violet shade deepens. Worn out.

For years I've wanted to live according to everyone else's morals. I've forced myself to live like everyone else, to look like everyone else. I said what was necessary to join together, even when I felt separate. And after all of this, catastrophe came. Now I wander amid the debris, I am lawless, torn to pieces, alone and accepting to be so, resigned to my singularity and to my infirmities. And I must rebuild a truth—after having lived all my life in a sort of lie.

At least the theatre helps me. The parody is better than the lie: it is closer to the truth that it performs.

May.

Resumed work. Have progressed with the first part of *First Man.* Recognition of this country, of its solitude, of its beauty.

May 13.

Travel to Arles. M. Pentecôte's splendid youth; travel to Toulon.

Television broadcast.[3] I cannot "appear" now without causing reactions. Remember, repeat to myself, constantly, that I must eliminate all unproductive polemic. Exalt all which must be. Silence the rest. If I do not hold myself to this rule, in the current state of things, I must agree to pay and be punished. See stages of healing.[4] Hang on to this precious tremor, this total silence that I have found here. The rest does not matter.

For almost five years I have been critical of myself, of what I believed, of what I lived. This is why those who share the same ideas believe themselves to be the target, and bear such an intense grudge against me; but no, I wage war with myself and I will destroy myself, or I will be reborn, that is all.

The Marseillais lovers. Under the beautiful sky, the juicy sea, the gaudy and colorful city, their desire always renewed, tiresome at first and finally throwing them into an endless intoxication. . . . Only the creeks, white stones, and sea ablaze with light are chaste.

Grenier. Ermitages Maronites (Un Été au Liban).[5] "In the same cave, one sees almost effaced—and it is a pity—a small,

---

[3] This is in regard to the *Gros plan* televised on May 12, 1959, which can be found in the Plélade volume "Théâtre-récits et nouvelles," page 1720, under the title "Pourquoi je fais théâtre."

[4] See page 203.

[5] "Ermitages Maronites" ("Maronites Retreat") is a chapter in *Un Été au Liban* (*A Summer in Lebanon*), a text with which Jean Grenier completed, in 1962, his *Lettres d'Égypte* (*Egyptian Letters*), published by Gallimard in 1950.

much older crucifixion where Christ, knees half bent, seems to wear bouffant pants like the country's inhabitants—and it is accompanied by strangelo lettering (what is Strangelo)." To write beneath the title – Le Strangelo—a not quite comprehensible narrative.

May 21.
    This is the red season. Cherries and poppies.

At noon the sound of a tractor in the small valley of Lourmarin . . . Like that of the boat's engine in the port of Chios, overpowered by the heat, and I was in the shade-filled cabin, waiting; yes, like today, full of a love without object.[6]
    I love the small lizards, as dry as the stones where they run. They are like me, of skin and bone.

Paris, June '59.
    I have abandoned the moral point of view. Morals lead to abstraction and to injustice. They are the mother of fanaticism and blindness. Whoever is virtuous must cut off the heads. But what to say of those who profess morality without being able to live up to its high standards. The heads fall and he legislates, unfaithful. Morality cuts in two, separates, wastes away. One must flee morality, accept being judged and not judging, saying yes, creating unity—and for the time being, suffering agony.

Danoise de Joski.
The city drunk with heat.

[6] Reference to the June 1958 boat trip to Greece with Michel Gallimard.

Venice from July 6 to July 13.[7]

The heavy and dead heat, like an enormous sponge, was crushing the lagoon, cutting the hideaway from the side of the Pont de la Liberté and, installed above the city, weighed on it, obstructing the outlets of the streets and canals, filling all the free space between the closely situated houses. No exit door, no escape, a heat trap where we must live and go round in circles. An army of hideous tourists turned thus, furiously, crazed, sweating, savage, dressed grotesquely, like the terrible troupe of an immense circus, suddenly idle and terrified to be so. The whole city was drunk with heat. In the morning we read in Il Gazzattino that some Venetians, driven crazy by the heat, had been sent to the insane asylum. Exhausted cats were everywhere. Occasionally one of them rose, risking a few steps on the burning campo, and at once the soft and malicious sun, which was on the lookout, knocked it down. Rats hoisted themselves above the canals' stagnant waters and three seconds later fell back into the water en masse. This soft and burning heat seemed to eat away at the increasingly decrepit city, the peeling splendor of the palaces, the burning campos, the moldy foundations and piles of mooring, and Venice plunges a little deeper into the lagoon.

We wandered, for our part, unable to eat, and we nourished ourselves with coffees and ice creams, unable to sleep, and we no longer knew where the days and nights began and ended. The day surprised us on the Lido beach, in the tepid and viscous morning water, or on a gondola wandering in the lost canals while the sky became a greyish pink above the suddenly turquoise tiles. The city was empty then, but the heat did not let up, neither at this hour nor in

---

[7] During a tour, *The Possessed* plays at the Fenice, in Venice, where Camus himself sets up the stage.

the evening hour, always steady, always burning and humid, and Venice has always been surrounded, while, giving up hope of ever leaving, we looked only to breathe one more time, and another still, in short to last in this strange time without landmarks nor rest, nerves on edge from coffee and insomnia, torn from life. Beings beyond time, but beings, likewise, that no one, nor anything in the world, desired other than in the continuation of this crazed and immobile insanity, in the center of the frozen fire that devoured Venice, hour after hour, endlessly, and at this point where we waited for the instant when suddenly the city, earlier still glittering with colors and beauty, would sink into ashes, which not even the absent wind would carry away. We waited, hanging on to one another, unable to separate ourselves, burning also, but with a sort of interminable and strange joy, on this pyre of beauty.

D.J. notices a young Danish girl, incidentally rather ugly, on the terrace of a café and then in the theatre. He approaches her, sits next to her, then a few moments pass, then they get up together. My heart aches seeing the submissive air with which she follows him. That submissiveness that they all have at this moment.

It is there that J. informs me that she is pregnant by P.; I advise her to talk to him about it. He laughs and an hour later returns to his hotel with X., in front of J. J. remains with X., who likes her, and falls silent.

Novel. Love bursts between them as a passion of flesh and heart. Days and days vibrant, and a total blending to the point where the flesh becomes sensitive and touched like the heart. United everywhere, in the sailboat, and continuous desire reborn as emotion. For him it is a struggle against death, against himself, against oblivion, against her and her weak nature, and finally he gives up, goes back between her hands. And after her there will be nobody else, he knows it, promises it in the only place he finds slightly sacred. At Saint Julien the Poor, where Greece joins with Christ, he decides to keep this promise despite everything, so that behind this being whom he clutches against him, there is only emptiness, and he clutches her tighter and tighter, melting into her, opening her up until the agonizing struggle to at last take refuge, sheltering himself there forever, in the love finally recovered, the place where the senses themselves sparkle in the light, purify him on an unremitting pyre, or a jubilant gushing water—crowning themselves with a limitless gratitude. This hour where the borders of bodies fall, where the singular being is finally born in the total nakedness of profound benefaction.

August 13.

Absence, painful frustration. But my heart is alive, my heart is finally alive. So it was not true that indifference had overcome everything. Gratitude, fiery acknowledgment to Mi. Yes, jealousy testifies for the spirit. It's the pain of seeing the other reduced to an object and the desire that everyone and everything acknowledge it as subject. One is not jealous of God.

Evening fell on the small valley, the old walls, the crenels, the patient houses. The rustling of the grass beneath my feet.

September.

Y. Printemps awakens at 11 o'clock, stays in bed, lunches in bed around 1 or 2 o'clock, and then stays in bed until the end of the afternoon surrounded by France-Dimanche, Match, Noir et Blanc, Cinémonde,[8] etc., etc., which she devours.

Mi, to whom I speak, half-laughing, half-serious, of extreme old age, when the flight of things is finished, of the jubilation of the senses, etc., bursts into sobs, "I love love so much!"

Before writing a novel, I'll put myself in a state of darkness for years. Test of daily concentration, intellectual asceticism, and extreme lucidity.

Culpability of a people? (France like Germany – Judas—those who lie idle, etc.).

How is your dear mother? I was pained to lose her 3 months ago. Oh, I was unaware of that detail.

One hundred forty thousand dying per day; ninety-seven per minute; fifty-seven million in one year.

This left that I belong to, in spite of me and in spite of it.

---

[8] A traditional list of well-known French news and film magazines.

The death that began in Adam ends in Christ.

The most exhausting effort in my life has been to suppress my own nature in order to make it serve my biggest plans. Here and there—here and there only—have I succeeded.

For the mature man, only happy loves can prolong his youth. Other loves throw him suddenly into old age.

Unfortunate to reach the age of responsibilities without the loss of sensibility that usually corresponds to it and then allows for the exercising of these responsibilities without excessive regard for others.

M. Mathieu[9] retires from his position as a literature professor. To confront death there is only the recipe of classical humanism.

In the towns of stone the wind and rain bring only the memory of meadows and sky.

For me, physical love has always been bound to an irresistible feeling of innocence and joy. Thus, I cannot love in tears but in exaltation.

---

[9] In 1932, M. Mathieu was Camus' literature professor in *premiere superieure*.

The sea, divinity.

Over the primitive ground the rains have been falling *for centuries* in an uninterrupted manner.

It is in the sea that life is born, and for all of time immemorial, which has led life from the first cell to the organized marine creature, the continent, without animal or plant life, was only a land of stones filled solely with the sound of wind and rain in the center of an enormous silence, traversed by no movement other than the rapid shade of large clouds and the racing waters over the ocean basins.

After billions of *years* the first living being exited the sea and set foot on terra firma. It looked like a scorpion. This was three hundred and fifty million years ago.

The flying fish make their nests in the abysses so as to shelter their eggs there.

In the Sargasso Sea, two million tons of algae.

The large red jellyfish, at first the size of a thimble, in the springtime becomes broad like an umbrella. It moves by pulsations, trailing behind it long tentacles and sheltering under its parasol clusters of codfish that move along with it.

The fish that climbs higher than its habitat, passes an invisible border, bursts, and falls to the surface.

The deep sea squid, unlike those of the surface, which emit an ink, emit a luminous cloud. They hide themselves in the light.

Terra firma, finally, is nothing but a very thin plate on the sea. One day the ocean will reign.

There are waves that reach us from Cape Horn after a trip of ten thousand kilometers. The tidal wave of 358 rose in the eastern Mediterranean, submerging the low islands and coasts and leaving the fishing boats on the forts of Alexandria.

I am a writer. It is not I but the pen that thinks, remembers, or discovers.

I cannot live with people for a long time. I need a little solitude, a portion of eternity.

In the Grand Luberon, a domesticated horse, which has escaped, lives in freedom, alone for years. Short story? A man who has heard talk of it goes to look for it. He is converted to the free life.

For Nemesis (in Lourmarin December '59).

Black horse, white horse, a single hand of man controls the two passions. At breakneck speed, the race is joyous. Truth lies, frankness hides. Hide yourself in the light.

The world fills you and you are empty: plenitude.

Soft sound of foam on the morning beach; it fills the world as much as the clatter of fame. Both come from silence.

The one who refuses chooses himself, who covets prefers himself. Do not ask nor refuse. Accept surrender.

Flames of ice crown the days; sleep in the motionless fire.

Equally hard, equally soft, the slope, the slope of the day. But at the summit? a single mountain.

The night burns, the sun creates darkness. O earth that suffices at everything. Freed of everything, enslaved to yourself. Enslaved to others: freed of nothing. Select your servitude.

Behind the cross, the devil.[1] Leave them together. Your empty altar is elsewhere.

The waters of pleasure and of sea are equally salty. Even within the wave.

The exiled individual reigns, the king is on his knees. In the desert, solitude ceases.

On the sea, without truce, from port to island, running in the light, above the liquid abyss, joy, as long as very long life.

You mask yourself, here they are naked.

In the brief day that is given to you, warm and illuminate, without deviating from your course.

Millions of other suns will come for your rest.

On the flagstones of joy, the first slumber.

Sowed by the wind, reaped by the wind, and creative nonetheless, such is man, through the centuries, and proud to live a single instant.

"The vanity of men erects these magnificent mansions only to receive the inevitable host there, Death, with all the ceremonies of superstitious awe" (Conrad, Anguish).

Saint Ignace (spiritual journal) "indignant" not to receive from the heavens confirmation of his election by the Holy Trinity. But he wished "to die with Jesus rather than live with another."[2] Hell would make him more unhappy by the blasphemy that is made of God's name than by the sufferings one endures there.

Id.: he tells the devil who tempts him: "Stay in your place." Elsewhere: that God is immutable and the devil immobile and changing.

---

[1] See page 244.

[2] Camus had already recorded similar statements of belief. In *The Rebel* he quotes Meister Eckhart who assures that he prefers hell with Jesus rather than heaven without him. In *The Possessed*, Stavrogin tells Shatov that, if one proved mathematically that truth is apart from Christ, he would rather remain with Christ than with truth.

For Don Faust.[3] There is no more Don Juan because love is free. There are men who please more than others. But neither sin nor heroism.

There is Lope de Vega's Don Juan: *La promesse accomplice* (translate it and also Zorrilla).[4] Philip IV's love for sister Marguerite de la Croix[5] (see the famous trials of Spain), see also (p. 189 and sq.) Don Juan and Gregorio Marañón's Don Juan.[6]

In "Parabole"[7] (p. 388) the one condemned to death who had said that he was innocent, then acknowledged that he was not, resigned himself. Then, beneath the noose, he sees a bird flying toward a branch and alighting there where it begins to sing; he seizes the noose then and shrieks that he is innocent.

Thus I have chosen you and this is what will help me pass this bad period, to no longer suffer from the details of what I recognize as just and legitimate in principle. . . .

---

[3] See Notebook VII, pages 95–96, and NNotebook VIII, pages 111, 134, 135, 171, 182, 195.

[4] José Zorrilla (1817–1893), Spanish poet and dramatist. His *Don Juan Tenorio* is a Romantic play where the doomed seducer is redeemed by the love of a woman. Since its creation, in 1844, this play has been staged in Spain every November 1.

[5] Philip IV fell in love with a pretty nun from the San Placido convent, in Madrid. To meet her, he dug a passage into the cellar of the convent. But the Mother Superior, warned by the nun, had organized a fake scene. The king found his beloved apparently dead, stretched out on a bed, eyes closed, surrounded by candles. He fled. Although the matter was suppressed, the Inquisition had been alerted and the scandal was huge.

[6] Gregorio Marañón (1887–1960), Spanish physician and writer who scientifically studied historical characters like Don Juan.

[7] *Parabole (A Fable)*, novel by William Faulkner (Random House, 1954), French translation by R. N. Raimbault (Gallimard, 1958).

What also helped me—equity—this difficult acceptance of oneself and others is creation. But since I am in this crisis, in this sort of impotence, I understand this ignoble desire for possession that, in others, has always incensed me. One can conquer a being for lack of being conquered oneself. And it is true that at precisely this moment, I have need of this belonging that you had given me. For this reason, as much as for your evasion, I have suffered from your lie. But this will pass. A little more pessimism still and unhappiness will radiate in turn: I will become myself again.

I have suffered from what you revealed to me: that's a fact. But you do not have to be sad for my sadness. I am wrong, I know it, and if I cannot prevent my heart from being unjust, I can at least make it capable of equity. It will not be difficult for me to overcome the injustice that I do to you in my heart. I know that I have done everything to detach you from me. All my life, as soon as a person got attached to me, I did everything to distance them. There is of course the incapacity wherein I am to make commitments, my taste for people, of multiplicity, my pessimism with regard to myself. But perhaps I was not as frivolous as I say. The first person whom I loved and I was faithful to escaped me through drugs, through betrayal. Maybe many things came from this, from vanity, from fear of suffering further, and yet I've accepted so much suffering. But I have in turn escaped from everyone since and, in a certain way, I wanted everyone to escape from me. Even X. I have done whatever necessary to discourage her. I do not believe that she escaped me, that she gave herself even fleetingly to another man. I am not sure [. . .].[8] But if she did not do it, it would

---

[8] One illegible word.

be because of a decision due to her inner heroism, not because of an overabundance of a love that wants to give without asking anything in exchange. So, I have done everything necessary in order for you to escape from me. And the more the captivation of that September increased, the more I wanted to break a certain enchantment. Thus, in a certain way, you have escaped me. That is the sometimes awful justice of this world. Betrayal answers betrayal, the mask of love is answered by the disappearance of love. And in this particular case, I, who have claimed and lived all liberties, I know and I recognize that it is right and good that, in your turn, you have lived one or two liberties. The count is not even complete.

To help myself, in any case, I will not only help myself to this cold equity of the heart but to the preference, to the tenderness, that I carry for you. I sometimes accuse myself of being incapable of love. Maybe this is true, but I have been able to *select* a few people and to keep for them, faithfully, the best of me, no matter what they do.

AFTERWORD

IN THE final weeks of December 1959, Albert Camus told his friend Urbain Polge: "What pleases me is that I have finally found the cemetery where I will be buried. I will be fine there." Struggling with his writing, Camus sent a letter to Catherine Sellers in which he wrote: "To work, one must deprive oneself, and die without aid. So let's die, because I don't want to live without working. . . ." On December 30 he wrote a line to Maria Casarès regarding his return to Paris, which, had the line been written in one of his novels, would certainly have seemed to stretch believability: "Let's say [Tuesday] in principle, taking into account surprises on the road. . . ."[1]

And it was on the road, five days after those words were written—January 4, 1960—that the dashboard clock of Michel Gallimard's 1959 Facel Vega HK 500 stopped ticking at 1:55 P.M. The clock lay in a nearby field. Fragments of the wreckage spread almost five hundred feet. A tire sat alone on the scarred cement. Drizzle dotted the road. A black leather valise lay in the mud, tossed next to the tree around which the car was wrapped.

---

[1] All of the above letters and quotations were collected and reprinted in Oliver Todd's *Albert Camus: Une Vie*. The English-language edition, *Albert Camus: A Life*, is heavily edited, containing approximately half the original text material. The above translations, derived from the first French edition, are my own.—R.B.

Wedged into the back windshield of the wrecked automobile was the body of Albert Camus, a long scratch etched along his forehead, his eyes stretched open. Killed instantly. Official cause of death: "fracture of the skull and spinal column."

He was forty-six.

In time, Camus' mud-caked valise was returned to his wife, Francine. When she opened the briefcase—Camus never used the lock—she found several items of note, including a French translation of Nietzsche's *The Gay Science* and a copy of Shakespeare's *Othello*, also in a French translation.[2] At the time of his death, it is believed Camus had begun working in earnest on his adaptation of the Shakespearean tragedy, as later, in a valise sent by train, Mme. Camus discovered a typed transcript of the play, which had her husband's handwritten revisions and markings throughout the first three acts.[3]

Nonetheless these books were not the most important items in the muddy briefcase. Among Camus' passport, personal photographs, and letters, also inside the valise was the last volume of these Notebooks (IX), which he carried with him, literally, until his death. And then there was, perhaps, the biggest discovery: *Le Premier Homme*,[4] the largely autobiographical novel that Camus had hoped would be his big book, his *War and Peace*. When it was recovered there were 144 pages, an incomplete first draft, scrawled in his small, tight script, often without periods or commas. For years this draft remained behind closed doors. It was not until 1994, thirty-seven years after the French journal *Arts*

---

[2] As can be seen in these Notebooks, and elsewhere, Camus held a high reverence for Shakespeare, even, perhaps tellingly, naming his car Desdemona, after Othello's wife.

[3] It is not known for certain who composed the typed transcript Camus was making notes on, but it seems possible that Catherine Sellers, who spoke fluent English and was familiar with Shakespeare's works, might have had some part in it.

[4] *The First Man.*

sarcastically wrote of Camus, "'Le Nobel couronne une œuvre terminée,"[5] that the general public would finally be offered a glimpse of this last unfinished manuscript and see for themselves that *Arts* had been wrong.

In her introduction to the American edition of *Le Premier Homme*, Camus' daughter, Catherine, acknowledged the hostile attitudes toward her father, which seemed to permeate France at the time, as one of the main reasons the manuscript was not published sooner. But when the manuscript was finally published, instead of drawing the censure of past political foes, the book met with widespread critical acclaim, showing *Arts* and other politically motivated critics that Camus clearly had much left to contribute. Even though, after winning the Nobel Prize, only *The Possessed* and a handful of essays were published while he was still alive, we can see in *Le Premier Homme* the promise that Camus' best work may have been yet to come.

In addition to *Le Premier Homme*, we can see in these Notebooks the beginnings of several projects Camus had planned and begun taking notes for. There were the two plays: one concerning the life of Julie de Lespinasse and the other attempting to blend the legend of Don Juan, which had preoccupied Camus for much of his life, with that of Faust. Then there was the essay on Nemesis, who Camus saw as the goddess of moderation and on whom he had planned to center his next major writing cycle. Like the previous cycles—the first on the absurd, the second on revolt—this cycle on love was to involve a play, a novel, and an essay.

Ultimately, though, none of these works would be completed. At the point where he may have been at the top of

---

[5] "The Nobel Crowns a Finished Work." Winning the Nobel Prize in 1957, at age forty-four, Camus became the youngest Frenchman to win the prize and the second-youngest recipient overall (Rudyard Kipling won the prize at age forty-two). Given Camus' relative youth at the time, the *Arts* proclamation seems especially biting.

his craft, Camus was removed from the world, and we were thus forced to accept, as Jean-Paul Sartre wrote in his *Tribute to Albert Camus*, that "every life that is cut off—even the life of so young a man—is at one and the same time a phonograph record that is broken and a complete life."[6]

Camus sensed the immediacy and constant presence of death around him—he knew all too well that his lungs would likely not allow him to live to old age—but with the many weights bearing on him at the time, what he might not have been so sure of, what we now know, what we see clearly, is that his voice, like the last words of his Caligula, is *still alive* and will continue to live long past his shortened life.

[6] See *The Reporter*, February 4, 1960, page 34.